MW01687999

LAN B
BR 124 H53
Doubting castle / Hie
33109001560671

BR 124 .H53
Hiebert, P.
Doubting castle.

WITHDRAWN

Doubting Castle

Paul Hiebert,

M.A., M.Sc., Ph.D., L.L.D., D.Lit., F.C.I.C.

Vancouver Community College
Langara - Library
100 West 49th Avenue
Vancouver, British Columbia
V5Y 2Z6

Q

Queenston House Publishing Inc.
102 Queenston Street
Winnipeg, Manitoba
Canada

JUN 10 1977

Grateful acknowledgement is made to the Manitoba Arts Council and the Canada Council for grants to aid in the publication of this book.

Copyright © 1976 by Queenston House Publishing, Inc.

All rights reserved. No part of this book may be reproduced or transmitted in any form, electronic or mechanical, including photography, recording or any information storage and retrieval system without permission in writing from the publisher.

Canadian Cataloguing in Publication Data

Hiebert, Paul, 1892—
Doubting castle

ISBN 0-919866-15-8

1. Christianity - 20th century. 2. Hiebert, Paul, 1892— I. Title.

BR124.H53 201 C76-016061-9

Printed in Canada by Hignell Printing Limited,
Winnipeg, Manitoba. Canada

Neither could they, with all the skill they had, get again to the stile that night. Wherefore, at last, lighting under a little shelter, they sat down there until the day-break; but, being weary, they fell asleep. Now there was, not far away from the place where they lay, a castle called Doubting Castle, the owner whereof was Giant Despair; and it was in his grounds they were now sleeping: wherefore he, getting up in the morning early, and walking up and down in his fields, caught Christian and Hopeful asleep in his grounds. They told him that they were pilgrims, and that they had lost their way.

*****

Now when they were gone over the stile, they began to contrive with themselves what they should do at that stile, to prevent those that should come after, from falling into the hands of Giant Despair. So they consented to erect there a pillar, and to engrave upon the side thereof this sentence – "Over this stile is the way to Doubting Castle, which is kept by Giant Despair, who despiseth the King of the Celestial Country and seeks to destroy his holy pilgrims.

From Bunyan's *Pilgrim's Progress.*

CONTENTS

Last night I walked with God. He said,
Well, Stranger it's been quite a while,
Just where on earth have you been wandering now–
Lost, I suppose; that restless search of yours
To find yourself must take you far afield –
But then I need not ask, I know full well
Just how distressing now earth's valleys seem,
Fearsome and dark and lonely – haunted too
By guilt and ghosts – though loneliness is worst –
But tell me, Friend, what brings you back to me?

Lord, I said, the fault is mine I know,
But also yours, you planted that damned tree
Of good and evil square across my path –
Tell me, Lord, did you expect of me
That I could pass it each and every day,
And never ask, what's this forbidden fruit,
This evil I am not supposed to know,
Whose knowledge of the good is even vague?

Friend, said God, it was not forbidden fruit,
I merely warned you of its consequence,
For knowledge is experience, not words;
I gave you freedom so that you could love,
And in your loving you could be like me,
To be like God, not gods, was yours to choose,
For freedom given cannot be constrained –
The choice was yours – and if not free,
There was neither good nor evil in the tree.

Introduction

One of the greatest joys in the adventure of life is that of discovery, the discovery of some place or scene of which one has heard and read – to find it finally brought within the reality of experience. I am thinking, for example, of such places as, say, the Grand Canyon of Arizona or Lake Louise in Alberta. One drives for hours over an indifferent desert road or winds around and around an unimpressive mountain and then suddenly – there it is! Of course, such places were there all the time awaiting a personal discovery. They were expected and one was, as it were, searching for them, but to have them revealed in such surprising reality, spread out in awe and wonder is one of the traveller's greatest delights. I have had many such experiences and have never lost my joy in them, perhaps all the more because as a boy growing up in a bleak little prairie town at the turn of the century I had little expectation of ever travelling to far-away places. London, Paris, the cow-boy country of romantic reading, the battle fields of our history books, of actually seeing Kings and Queens and rajahs, of meeting writers and scientists who were famous, such were the things of which only dreams were made.

But life unfolds and has been very rich. Dreams have come true. Looking back after a long and abundant life, I am convinced, however, that the greatest and loveliest realities discovered are those of the mind and spirit because that which is revealed there is ultimate and enduring beyond the waste and corrosion of time and process. Like those scenes and places of adventurous travel, they were always there for discovery and one searches for them. In the end they too were revealed to the soul as the landscapes were revealed to the eye. But the desert roads to them were often more dreary and the mountain road steeper and more torturous. One travels in search of spiritual Truth much as one travels in search of scenic vistas and grandeurs, and although the way itself is beset with anxieties and apprehensions and sometimes with despairing doubt of ever reaching anywhere – indeed for all of us it is to a greater or lesser extent the way of the cross – in the end the reward of reaching happy uplands flooded in the light of God's love is greater than all the lovely experience of life which memory can fill.

Doubting Castle tells something of the desert roads and the winding paths within my own life leading to the clearer vision and wider outlook on reality. It is a sharing of experience with those who travel the same way.

P.G.H.

What is Truth?

In one way or another we are all searching for the meaning of life. In a way, we are all searching for the good life, but the life which is not meaningful is not good. Some of us may not be looking for any particular meaning; we do not feel that we have to have any rational and coherent philosophy in which the meaning of life may be found. The problem seems to be answered, if it arises at all, by whatever present satisfaction is reached in the process of living. Pleasure, material comfort, achievement, acclaim, ambitions realized, fulfilment in one form or another is often regarded as an aim and object in itself and no further meaning is required. But in the end we cannot escape the larger problem of meaning because of life's temporality. Death closes the door upon every achievement and satisfaction. The light that was turned on at one end is turned off at the other and all of life's activity becomes meaningless because the time element in which it had its existence is no longer there.

When we reflect upon this destruction of our realities and our values, and this applies to all things we hold dear, persons as well as possessions, we cannot help searching for some system of truths, or some larger area of Truth, in which we may indeed find a meaning of life beyond its temporality. We look indeed for a greater Truth in which all of the little truths encountered in our daily lives have their significance.

I don't suppose we would search for Truth at all

if we were not faced with inevitable death and its accompaniments of pain and sorrow. "What is Truth," might never arise in our thoughts unless it were forced upon us. The ancient writer of the Book of Genesis, who so poetically pictured man as having once lived in happy contentment in Eden before he had eaten of the Tree of Knowledge, had the insight to realize that to eat thereof would at once launch man into the search for Truth beyond the evil perceived in his new knowledge. We cannot conceive of Adam, who in the evenings "walked with God," ever asking him in the course of their stroll: "What is Truth?" But now that has become the big question in our lives, and poets and priests and philosophers throughout the ages have been trying to find the answer.

We are told that Truth and beauty are closely related. Or again, we are told that many things which bother us here become clear in the light of Truth. Moreover we are told that the Truth shall make us free. Even Jesus, on one occasion, speaks of himself as being, "the Way, the Truth, and the life," a most remarkable statement which must have caused much puzzlement and some derision among the matter-of-fact Jews. But whatever our attitude toward Truth, this at least is sure: it is not the simple relationship between discovered facts as when we say that two and two makes four, or that scientifically the height of the tides depends on the position of the moon. Truth appears to be a context of meaning in which we strive to find the meaning of ourselves. In my own thinking and in my personal life I have come to the conclusion that what we call knowledge of Truth is actually to discover the nature of God and that the knowledge of Truth can never be complete in our present lives. All we can hope for is to widen our angle of perception.

One of the interesting aspects of this search for Truth is that, although there seems to be a universal awareness that there is such a thing, there seems at the same time to be a great denial of it, which may have arisen out of a frustrated search. Pilate comes at once to mind since his famous "What is Truth?" uttered in the face of the very one who claimed to embody it, has echoed and re-echoed through the centuries.

I always feel a little sorry for Pilate – certainly I have sympathy for him. He seems to have been a decent Roman with a reasonable sense of justice, perhaps a slight cynicism, and a sense of disillusionment. I always think of him as having the tolerance of mind which comes from lack of conviction, or as one who could accommodate himself to circumstances if it were to his advantage to do so. If he had lived during the last war he would have been a "collaborator." He may have had a sense of justice but he had no passion for it, and the fact that he should have dismissed the whole problem of Truth by a somewhat embittered remark, "What is Truth?" leads me to believe that as a product of Roman culture and some education, he had at one time or another pondered the question of truth and had given it all up as a futile search.

History may never forgive Pilate, but I believe that in the matter of God's mercy he is as open to it as any of the rest of us. In the matter of the condemnation of Christ he played his practical politics, but without that vindictive hatred of the High Priests who were Christ's accusers. They did not ask themselves, "What is Truth?" They were very assured of knowing it, so completely assured that in their opinion no deviation from it was possible, and, although there may have been some among them who were not vindictive and full of hatred, their conviction of being in possession of Truth was so complete that they must have felt that anything beyond its circumscribed limits should be coldly rooted out. I have learned from my own experience that the assurance of rightness within one's self can so easily become self-righteousness, which is the brother of arrogance and intolerance.

If I have a sympathy for Pilate, I also have for Judas, that silly man. Because in my own life the search for Truth has been so difficult and at many stages so unsatisfying, I do not think for a minute that Judas was the crafty villain which my early religious teachings made him out to be. I don't think that the discerning Christ would ever have chosen him as a member of the twelve if he had been that. I think he was a man of good will, a materialist and probably a humanist whose idea of the good was the social good, but who, like Pilate in his contemplation of Truth, became disillusioned and decided that Christ was an impractical idealist whose gospel would never be accepted and whose ideas would never work. So he surrendered his Master to the authorities – the "state" in our terms or to what we would call "society." Moreover, like Pilate, he was not above the making of a bit of advantage out of his defection. He certainly had no idea that he was selling Christ to his death by his act, and when he discovered the enormity of his deed the next day his remorse overwhelmed him to the point of suicide.

Now Pilate and Judas and the High Priests are still with us and have been with us throughout recorded history. One need not be particularly astute in an analysis of the social scene to find their modern counterparts. But they win our sympathy in that they are all in a manner concerned with Truth according to their own lights although in most cases what they regard as Truth is merely a satisfactory acceptance of whatever happens to serve the immediate purpose of their lives. Truth for them is happiness, or satisfaction in its various forms, and they are content to have it thus. But there are many of us who are looking for a final meaning, the why and wherefore of things and, above all, the why and wherefore of our own lives. The search for Truth is a search for meaning, for the purpose and destiny of life and the overcoming of the anomalies which stand in the way of the good life.

This book might well be called "An Adventure into Truth" or perhaps "Toward Truth," for I no longer believe, as I once did, that Truth is something one can overtake and seize upon and encompass with the mind. I do not any longer believe that Truth lends itself to finality in the sense in which those many little truths of our daily lives lend themselves to certainty. We recognize certain truths as facts and we are continually trying to see God in factual terms. But the Truth which makes us free, the Truth which, as Christ tells us, makes us whole, is beyond factual experience. It is the larger context in which the little truths of experience can be fitted and in which they have their meaning. This is particularly true in the course of our daily lives in finding the meaning of pain and sorrow as well as the happiness of love and beauty.

No one can say with absolute certainty: "I am right and you are wrong." We know very well how the arrogant assertion of being right has led to quarrels and cruelty. The religious wars and the tortures of the Inquisition come to mind. The so-called beliefs which hold people apart, the creeds and doctrines which have divided churches are not statements of ultimate Truth, though they generally profess to be, but are merely rationalizations arising out of an incomplete point of view, a narrower or wider angle whereby only certain aspects of Truth, and of God in whom all Truth lies, is seen. But the angle of vision, the seeing as well as the limitation of sight, lies not in the Truth we assert or in the God we profess to see. It lies, as I have said, in our training and talents and temperament whereby we select certain aspects of it to meet our personal needs. But, in the end we must see Truth beyond ourselves and overcome our natural tendency to see it only in our own terms.

I have devised in this connection a little parable of my own. It concerns three men who take a morning stroll through a meadow. It is a lovely morning and they all enjoy the sunshine and are thankful to God for the privilege of seeing and enjoying. But each brings to the experience a different point of view, a view which as good men they are willing to share with others. The two artists paint pictures, each beautiful in itself but nevertheless different. Moreover they paint these pictures not to make money or to become famous, but as true artists to call attention to certain colours and nuances in composition and effects which would normally not be observed. The true artist is always a sharer, one who reveals to others those things which his training and endowments have enabled him to see. He is saying in effect: "See it as I have seen it. Let me point out to you certain aspects which have given me joy and which you may overlook; it is my privilege as an artist to call your attention to certain beauties. I have been favoured with talents of perception and even revelation which I am endeavouring to pass on if you will accept them."

But notice again that both artists paint different pictures. They not only see differently but they select different details of what they have seen and to which they would call attention. The one artist's scale of artistic values is not the same as that of his fellow artist yet both are high in their revelation of beauty and they are both reaching out to the response which their artistic efforts undertake to elicit.

Now the man who sells real-estate is also a high-minded man. He could see possibilities in the meadow for profit to himself, but he is a humanitarian. He sees this undeveloped land as a housing opportunity for the poor and he may write a report about his walk through the meadow in which he points out the opportunity for a better life for the underprivileged, that is, cheap land. He also, like the artist, shares his point of view with his fellow men. All three of these men have a concern for others but each sees the meadow from his own angle or according to the scale of values in which he thinks, but the differences between them are not differences in Truth, but in those particular angles and aspects from which they approach it.

And so it is with our opinions and beliefs and doctrines concerning God whose nature we would undertake to understand. I think that what we call Truth is the growing understanding of the nature of God. Of course, when we attempt to rationalize our understandings, which are always limited because of our own limitations, we tend to put into words and formulas and doctrines our personal approach. But faith does not lend itself to the confined limitations of words and formulas. Faith can never be encompassed within the restriction of specific beliefs. Nevertheless, whenever we undertake to share with others those insights and revelations concerning God and Truth which come to us in the same manner as the revelation of beauty comes to the artist, we are immediately confined to our medium of expression as the artist is confined to the paint of his canvas. And just as in the case of the painting where a certain dab of green paint is a symbol which "stands for" a leaf on a tree, so in any discussion certain words are symbols which stand for ideas which in turn point to the Truth we hope to understand. But to interpret the word-symbols correctly we must in a measure enter into the personality of the author. Only thus can we know the meaning which he had in mind in using them or devising them into certain combinations and structures. We must, in fact, identify ourselves with the author or artist to receive his true meaning. In the end we must identify ourselves with God if we are to understand his creations in which we also are included.

This book is certainly not one of these tolerant and open-minded expositions which allows of any belief simply because it makes concessions to individual views. Indeed, it is an altogether fundamentalist book in its insistence upon the belief in God, and the growth of that belief into the acceptance of God as revealed in his Son. But as a scientist I am suspicious of 'facts'. And I am especially suspicious of literal facts which are adduced in support of some particular creed and dogma or some system of beliefs. These so often stand in the way of our entrance into God's Kingdom. Moreover, I have had so much difficulty and suffered so much spiritual distress in my own efforts to escape from the narrowness and legalisms which so-called facts presented and which were taught to me as God's final truth, that I would not undertake to lay down any dictates of my own. All I undertake to do here is to give an account of my own adventures into Truth in the hopes that others who tread the same path may recognize some of the same difficulties which I have experienced and feel comfortable in knowing that they are not alone and that in spite of their individual troubles of mind and spirit there is a universality under God. Comfort and understanding is thus extended from one to another.

That is why I call this book *Doubting Castle*. It is autobiographical in that it tells, out of my own experiences, how growth and progress may come about so that what was once fear becomes joy, and what was rules and restraint becomes freedom. But the heights to which one climbs in life's adventure in search of Truth is often a hard way in which doubts and guilt and dead-ends and frustrations mark the path; these may be forgotten once the high plateau has been reached from which one can now say with confidence, "Here it is as I see it." Our fellow travellers may then be overlooked in the new freedoms and achievements, but in the end one must share the distress and difficulties as well as the triumphs. It is not so much a matter of revealing discovery as of pointing the way toward where the discovery lies. I know that in my own life when I have so often been depressed and discouraged because I could not see through that dark glass of which the Apostle Paul speaks, I would come across some book, or some passage in a book, which would enable me to see the light and go ahead. The Doubting Castle which Christian discovered in Bunyan's *The Pilgrim's Progress* was occupied by "A Giant whose name was Despair." I too have sometimes felt that I was a prisoner in that castle, and I write this book since I too have known it and, like Christian, I have escaped.

The curse of the intellectual is doubt. I do not consider myself an intellectual, although I am sure I may have thought so when I was a sophomore at college. But intellectual or not I have spent the greater part of my life among the so-called intellectuals and if they do not suffer from doubts it is because they have so often surrendered themselves to a self-satisfying unbelief which does not rest upon any particular conviction of Truth or upon a sense of knowing, but upon denial. Having no convictions they tend to believe in almost everything, expecially that no-cause principle known as probability. Living within an atmosphere in which such things as having a belief in God is regarded with tolerant disdain, since it departs from the accepted attitude of those learned ones that the human mind is the last court of judgement in matters of truth, I often found that the young student entering the academic world had great difficulty in maintaining his belief and with it his faith in God. There is always a strong tendency to accept the attitude and outlook of the society in which we find ourselves at home, and there is also the fact that many of the teachings of childhood, and Sunday School, cannot stand up in the fact of modern learning. A spiritual vacuum is left in which no meaning beyond material relationships can be found. It is the very opposite of a spiritual rebirth. It is the drift into a kind of nihilism in which the loves and sorrows and pleasures of life may still be experienced but which lacks any final meaning or destiny since under the non-belief in God the human mind is forced into the acceptance of an impersonal material process as the last word. This, the scientific outlook, I have also shared. In my last book† I made the remark which I think is very pertinent to our present condition and which I think bears repetition: "It is not science which forces us into apostasy, but apostasy which forces us into science." This is because the non-acceptance of a Personal God leaves us with nothing but an impersonal, mechanical system as a context in which to do our thinking. But the result is death of the spirit.

The Christian admonition to love the Lord, our God, with all our heart and soul *and mind* confers a sanction upon the intellect as a means of perceiving the wonder of God. It is one of the great satisfactions and joys of life to find, that within faith in God the universe is philosophically consistent and intellectually adequate in spite of the many objections which are brought against it by unbelievers. But to knit together the various threads of thought which so often seem tangled and at variance is by no means easy and one is continually assailed by doubts. Religion, science, and philosophy are so often regarded as standing in opposition to each other, and to bring them together into a coherent system of thought involves more than the mind. It involves the heart and the soul which the mind so often derides. It involves spiritual as well as intellectual growth, a kind of re-birth in which man, as a person, turns toward God also as a Person, and there finds the key which unlocks his mind and the

† *Tower in Siloam*

context in which the mind can function. The wages of sin may be death but I am convinced that the wages of sin are also ignorance, a blocking of the mental faculties standing in the way of growth.

Frontier Religion

The religion of my childhood was what might be called a "frontier religion" based upon the concept of a frontier God. I have known many fellow prairie dwellers, some who are writers and others non-writers who can tell about their early days in the homesteading west. They tell of their hardships in meeting conditions of the prairie frontier, how they faced up to the physical demands for survival, overcame cold and drought and the lack of the comforts to which many had been accustomed before coming west. In the long distances of the empty plains they faced much lonesomeness, and the history of the western prairies tells of some who failed and gave up the struggle. But most won out against the odds and now in our modern civilization with all its comforts and amenities they are able to look back upon their early hardships with a certain pride of achievement and even with nostalgic fondness. But they tell little about their frontier religion.

In my own case I cannot say that I faced any of the hardships of the prairie pioneers. I knew of them but they never entered into my own experience. My parents, Mennonite immigrants from South Russia, would tell me about the sod houses in which the first settlers lived in Manitoba or, going back to Russia, would tell of a famine there in which a handful of grain and some boiled nettles gathered in the field constituted a meal. My father would tell me about his own father cutting barley with a scythe and tieing it into sheaves by hand and being interrupted in his labours by having to lie down in the field from time to time until attacks of malaria passed off. Drought and floods and grasshoppers kept them poor for many years when they moved to Manitoba.

But I knew nothing of such things at first hand. Indeed, I have never known hardship of any kind, or wondered where my next meal was coming from, or whether I would be able to support myself after I had left the family. By the time I arrived on the scene, my father had reached a stage of comparitive affluence, and he owned what in those days was called a "general store" in a Canadian community. It was a little Manitoba town and I grew up, a Canadian boy, monolingual and unaware of any foreign roots or of any ethnic background different from those of my playmates at school.

Much of the prairie frontier still remained. There was virgin soil to be turned, homesteads to be filed on, and the living conditions were still primitive. That decade just before the turn of the century which I remember most vividly as my early childhood was in the transition phase of western prairie history in which the frontier was beginning to give way to modernity. The trains which came through the town still had wide smokestacks and screens to prevent prairie fires and their cars were joined with link and pin couplers. My father bought many carloads of buffalo bones which still lay on the fields and shipped them east to be used in the refineries or for bone meal. Families of Indians in carts drawn by a single shaginappe wandered into town from the near reservations and we boys used to welcome them at the town nuisance-grounds and watch them kill and skin a dog for their dinners and hang some of the flesh upon sticks to dry. They sold willow baskets and wild fruit to the townspeople and begged for food and milk for their unhealthy children, for they were miserably poor.

I have many reminiscences and could tell a great deal about a boy growing up in those early days of Manitoba, and they are reminiscences of the Huckleberry Finn and the Tom Sawyer type. But my concern here is not to recount experiences of those early days. They may have been in many aspects harsh and bleak, but a boy growing up under those conditions can still be very happy and indeed I was. That which was harsh and bleak and in which I was often unhappy was not a frontier environment but a frontier religion. Just as the settlers themselves had to make their way out of their difficult conditions into the comforts and amenities of present life, so I had to find my way out of a stern and forbidding religious teaching into a higher understanding and a serenity of Christian faith.

I suppose there had always been a strong streak of religiosity in my nature probably inherited from those far Anabaptists whose beliefs and piety had been kept alive by Mennonite ancestry. Certainly much seems to have been inherited – my father and all his brothers were great arguers and disputers and no two of the six belonged to the same church. They had a reputation of being God-haunted, and some of them also of being very hypocritical in their apparent piety. But on my mother's side there was a very genuine piety and much calm faith which rose above argument and doctrinal dispute. I remember her telling me how, in Russia, during one of the meteoric showers in the middle of the nineteenth century, her grandmother's family had gathered on their knees throughout the night on the village green calmly awaiting the coming of the Lord, for on that day, when the stars were to fall from heaven, the Son of Man was to come again in all his glory. But on the other hand I was told of some great-aunt or other, who, blind and on her deathbed, had insisted that the gold coins she had collected throughout her life be brought to her, and lovingly fingering them, had departed in peace.

Such are the cross currents of human nature and I was certainly heir to them. Disputes, speculations, fears, superstitions, were to a great extent my spiritual diet as a child. But to my mother, rich in love and as I now realize, rich also in human faults, I nevertheless owe one great treasure which I have never lost. It was the repeated teaching that I was never, but never, regardless of frustrations and uncertainties and doubts and temptations and all the spiritual ills which beset life, to abandon my belief in God. That I have had and that has never left me. My difficulties, my doubts, and my despairs, have never been due to lack of belief in a God but from ignorance of the Christian God of which frontier religion seemed singularly unaware. The fear of God is said to be the beginning of wisdom, and it may well be that whatever wisdom I have acquired has arisen out of the effort to escape the fear of that stern and punishing God of my early childhood. He certainly was a Fearsome Being and I was often much distressed.

I had a belief of sorts and I shall always be thankful for it. It was, at least, a starting point for future faith. I don't suppose any of my brothers and sister had any great joy in the thought of God's existence, either. Certainly I did not since we were told that he was watching us all the time and would punish us for our sins. The Methodist Sunday School which we attended stressed the joy of salvation and we were promised a happy time in Heaven providing we repented for all our misdeeds and were accordingly good enough to get there. We were told that it was a place which had gold streets and pearly gates but beyond that it seemed rather unattractive. Our concern was not so much to reach Heaven as to escape the eternal punishment which awaited us if we failed to obey the rules which God had laid down for our obedience. I was never able to discover why certain rules had been thus laid down, but then parents and teachers and adults generally were always laying down rules which we did not understand and our tendency to disobey them was due to the fact that we had "been born in sin."

My father was superintendent of the Methodist Sunday School and I am inclined to think that the Methodist Church, more than other churches in the town, tended to emphasize this sense of being born in sin and that salvation and repentance were very necessary. It always seemed to me that the Presbyterian boys and girls of the church across the street were more lighthearted and having a better time than I. It was true their chances of Heaven were considered to be less than ours, but this belief may have been due to the fact that my own family was particularly strict and God-fearing in the literal sense. But looking back I am inclined to think that this fearsome approach to God was that of the small towns and the prairie community generally around the turn of the century and years later I was to discover to my surprise that it still prevailed to a considerable extent in the town in which I spent my early boyhood. Indeed, it still prevails in the Prairie West, throughout that large region of Canada and America which has been described as "The Bible Belt."

I don't suppose I had ever given the matter much thought. One is simply inclined to take for granted that because great changes have taken place within one's self that the world of the past background must have changed also. Perhaps it has. In this modern age with its permissiveness and its "God is dead" cults and its increasing emphasis upon self-expression, there has undoubtedly been a falling away from the old beliefs, even to a discarding of beliefs entirely. But what I found on my return to the town after many years was that the old beliefs seemed to have changed very little. I could not help feeling that a great deal of the old cheerless "Methodism" of my childhood still lay like a shadow over the religious life of the community and that some of that old spirit which used to be characterized as "the odor of sanctity" still lingered. In this I may have been wrong. Perhaps it was simply that the return to the old homes and old scenes and the old associations of childhood revived old memories and the old impressions.

I may occasionally have driven through that little town of my childhood but I had never spent a full day there or talked with its people for a full seventy years. There had been little to ever call me back. All my boyhood school-mates had died or had moved away and although the two houses in which I had lived were still there, no one remembered me except a few of the old-timers whom I in turn no longer remembered. But it was still the place where I had played and gone to my first school as a boy and it brought back many memories and impressions. There were the same streets I had plodded on the way to school, there was still the creek on the edge of the town where we used to find snakes and collect birds eggs, there were still some of the old houses in which my school-mates had lived, the unchanged railway station where we used to watch the daily arrival of the train with its wide smoke-stack and its wheel hand-brakes on each car, there were still the stone buildings whose slow construction from field boulders we had watched after school, the grain elevators and the churches. Above all it was churches which most carried me back because ours was a very churchy family and religion, or at least what passed for religion in those days, was the dominant influence in my impressionable childhood.

The occasion for the invitation for me to revisit this little Manitoba town after so many years was not that I had been born there or that I was remembered as a former citizen. It was merely that a number of the local churches had decided to hold what their modern euphimism termed "A Confrontation," meaning, as I was later to discover, something very closely resembling an old time revival meeting which in the little prairie town at the turn of the century was an annual affair like the Uncle Tom's Cabin tent show and the regular circus.

As I said, no one there remembered me. But I had just written a book, *Tower in Siloam*, in which as a professor teaching one of the physical sciences at the University I had undertaken to deal with the problem of the physical world in relation to man in his search for meaning. It had started out as a purely scientific book but as it developed it became a very religious book, since its main thesis, which is also herein being stated, was that the physical world was composed of the "action principle" of modern scientific discovery and that this in turn was the dynamic expression of the underlying personality of God. The world, in fact, was the *Will of God in action*, and this "action" had taken on those structural configurations which we recognize as the physical world in which we live. "The World" had thus become flesh or, to state it in other terms, it had become what we regard as matter and energy. In the logical application of this idea the book led to an exposition of man's universe followed by the creation of man himself which the physical universe had anticipated as man's home. Creation had finally culminated in the man, Christ, who was the Son of God.

It was this emphasis upon the will and purpose of God in human history as well as in man's present environment which no doubt led to my being asked to join in the activity of the Confrontation.

Modern science is always, and quite rightly, suspect in religious circles, and I am inclined to think that the fact that I, as a man of science, should make use of the very newest in scientific discovery to refute the denial of God and the apostasy of modern thought was why I was being welcomed to the Confrontation as a repentant sinner. I was returning to the fold and I was being asked to "witness." The whole affair impressed me as being very much a return to what we used to sing about as the old-time religion if not actually a return to the old-time fundamentalism. In fact, the confrontation, despite such modern innovations as a rock-group to pound out the hymns, had much of the old revival meeting of my youth about it and was held, like this one, in the local skating rink. It seemed to me, perhaps wrongly, that the spiritual environment had changed little since those churchy days when I was a boy in that same town and I confess that I found myself somewhat out of sympathy with the movement which I was being asked to promote. There still seemed to be much of the old drive which I remembered from long ago, a kind of forcing of the spirit which seemed to depend more on fervour than on conviction.

Actually I now think, despite my feeling, that the community must have changed. I do not believe that half a century and more can have passed in these days of greater communication without a broadening of outlook and a deepening of insight into religious truth which was so lacking in my childhood. I had little opportunity during my short stay of discussing religion with people or of attending church services to discover to what extent the liberalism of modern thought had brought about changes. I am speaking here only of my own impressions, and I admit that they might have been wrong impressions, but I felt that the approach to God was still a forced one, that the sense of obligation and guilt which was so dominant in my own childhood training was still dominant in the religious life of the community and that the "brother, are you saved?" rally with its implied threat of punishment was still hanging like a cloud over the religious life of the gathering. What seemed to be lacking was the calm happiness which Christianity is supposed to bring. And although I mention this particular town and this particular community because they entered into my own experience, I am convinced that it is little different from the large number of similar towns and communities throughout Canada and America. Much of the harsh religious attitude of the turn of the century still clings to them, and because this harshness stands in the way of the Gospel of Christ there can be much spiritual distress.

We did not in those days have the distractions of cars and television, and, apart from the skating rink for the younger folk and the curling rink and perhaps the saloon for the men, there were few activities in the winter. But there was the church. Sunday saw the usual two services in addition to Sunday School in the afternoon and I had to attend them all. For the older members of the family there were choir practices and prayer meetings during the week and also some mysterious gatherings such as the Women's Auxiliary and the Epworth League which I never understood since they were not for me. Then there were "Revival" meetings from time to time at which religious fervour was raised to a high pitch and at which local sinners were sometimes constrained to come to the front and resolve henceforth to lead better lives "before it was too late." My brother and I always regarded these meetings as rather fun and although we were not really moved by the evangelistic expertise of the visiting firemen, we always joined fervently in the groans and amens where we felt it was required. I am inclined now to think that we did this more to annoy my father than from any conviction. He suspected us of amusing ourselves but could do nothing about it since he himself was a man who was easily moved by loud and fervent speech whether at a religious or a political meeting. I have no doubt that some modern psychologist could explain our behaviour as arising out of some deep-seated "father resentment" which may indeed be true, but it was done in good spirit and was our lighthearted way of getting back at him for his stern insistence that we tread the straight and narrow path. Whatever Truth was instilled into us as children was certainly not the truth that made us free.

In addition to the occasional revival meetings there were the usual visiting missionaries at special evenings at the church who would generally appear in the native dress of the country of their mission field. They would tell us about the lives of the poor heathen children in Ceylon or India or Darkest Africa, whom we tended to envy a little because of their carefree lives. But since they never got enough to eat, which in our young opinion was very sad, we always contributed the little flat Canadian five-cent pieces which had been given to us by our parents for that purpose. We certainly, being little savages ourselves in many respects, did not feel any great obligation toward them, religious or otherwise, but we dutifully contributed to the missions in the same spirit in which we dutifully "signed the pledge" at the annual temperance meeting which was regularly presented under the auspices of the local W.C.T.U.

These temperance meetings were fun, too. They were particular fun because they were always illustrated with large pictures in lurid colours and sometimes by lantern slides. To this day I know very well from the slides what happens to the human stomach in its progressive stages from the first drink where it has a pink lining to the dark purple and black mottling in the final stages of delirium tremens. The walls of the stomach shown in the pictures were always pulled back for all to see like curtains in the Victorian parlour windows. There were sometimes demonstrations showing what happens to a lump of sugar when placed in a glass of water in contrast to what happened to it in a glass of pure alcohol. It became at once obvious to our young minds that a stomach full of pure alcohol could not dissolve sugar, and we sternly resolved on that account not to drink pure alcohol, at least not with sugar.

But what chiefly impressed us at these temperance meetings was a more or less condensed version of *Ten Nights in a Bar Room*, a book with which we were all familiar since it was practically required reading in every good household. In this book, a young man, a miller's son if I recall rightly, having taken the fateful first drink, then becomes a drunkard in ten chapters and ends by throwing a whiskey bottle at his father. The utterly condemnatory "Frank Slade, you have murdered your father!" with which the book ends completely cuts this youth off from any hope of salvation. Among us children it was taken for granted that, whatever one's feelings toward one's father, murder would never be forgiven. Murder of one's father, like illicit sex, was not to be forgiven ever. So we regularly stepped forward and went through the routine of signing "The Pledge" in which we promised to abstain forever from "tobacco, profanity, and strong drink."

Even the village drunkard signed the pledge from time to time. Every community had its village drunkard just as every community had its village atheist. These, the local atheists, the deniers of the God who was supposed to have encouraged the whale to swallow Jonah and made the earth stand still at Joshua's command, may not have been as loudly vociferous as our present national ones who appear on television and radio, but they used the same arguments and raised the same objections. "The Age of the Loud Mouth," with which historians may characterize our present times, had not as yet arrived, but the difference between those times and ours was merely a matter of decibels in the matter of religious objection. There was the usual defiance of literalism and fundamentalism, and, on a higher level, the familiar argument, "Any God who will permit wars and famine and disease in his created world is not one to believe in." But regardless of any validity such an objection may have had, the questioning mind was regarded by the Church-goers as being not of God, but of the Tempter. A drunkard could always reform; he could take "The Gold Cure," which was the current cure for alcoholism in that day; or his wife could have him placed on the "Indian List," which meant that the local saloon keeper was forbidden to sell him liquor. The atheist, however, was generally considered to be beyond hope, unless, as sometimes happened, a good revival meeting brought him around to a better way of thinking.

Although my parents had originally been Mennonites, by the time I came on the scene they had become complete Methodists, probably because, as I later discovered, that except for pacifism there was little to choose between the two persuasions. Since my father was superintendent of the Sunday School it meant even more strict attendance for us as children. We lived on a corner with the Presbyterian church across the street on one side and the Baptist church on the other. There was a small Anglican church down the street and in the other direction there was our own Methodist church, which I remember to this day as being architecturally ugly. There were no other churches in the town. It was a white Anglo-Saxon Protestant community except for a few "half breeds" of Indian-French descent living on the other edge of the town and these were Catholics. The Catholics were a race apart; we saw nothing of them, except once in a while a priest would visit the settlement and he always attracted a following of little boys who were fascinated by his cassock as "the man in a skirt." What little I knew of the Catholics was largely negative since anti-Catholicism was deep in the Mennonite tradition and practically unchanged since the time of the Reformation. I don't suppose I was ever actually told that Catholics would not go to heaven when they died, but I certainly gathered the impression that their chances were very slim. Even the Anglicans came under my parents' condemnation. "Just too Catholic" was a judgment I heard more than once concerning one or other of them, and the fact that regimental and national flags were displayed in their churches excluded them entirely from Christian consideration. Methodists or not, our family was strongly pacifist.

About the Baptists in the town we seemed to have no definite opinions except perhaps that they were regarded as a bit queer. My own interest in them was confined to watching the men filling the baptismal tanks from the pump wagons which were otherwise used for the engines during the threshing season, and, on one occasion at least, watching the actual immersions and wondering how the baptized were going to get dry in the church. With the Presbyterians across the street we had a mild spiritual affinity and once in a while we would attend their services, especially, I think, because their minister lived next door and his wife became a very good friend of my mother. But on the whole our attitude toward the Presbyterians was one of cautious reserve, not so much because they were regarded as doctrinally wrong, but rather because they tended to be a more worldly group, giving greater attention to pleasure than to piety.

Our religion was nominally Christian but actually it was un-Christian. We were taught, of course, that Jesus had died for our sins, but to me at least that never carried much meaning since we were also taught that our sins were still being chalked up against us in a kind of good-and-bad ledger which could be opened on the last day for a final accounting. The God of my childhood was a capricious God who had laid down certain arbitrary rules. Sins against him thus consisted of definite acts. Those who avoided them were often given to self-righteousness and entertained the conviction that they stood in God's esteem. The matter of God's esteem did not greatly affect me personally – the threat of his punishment, even when not augmented by my parents, was enough to keep me reasonably on the straight and narrow path.

The truth is that we were never sorry for our sins – what child ever is? We were afraid of the consequences of our acts which were being called sins, but we did not know the meaning of sin because we did not know the meaning of Christian love. We never accepted Christ because our teaching was essentially un-Christian. Since the Bible was accepted as the literal word of God, the God therein was the God who had driven Adam and Eve from the Garden of Eden, not because of sin but because of disobedience. He was a God who drowned all the world except Noah and his family and had instructed the Israelites to invade Canaan and put men, women, and children to the sword if they resisted. He "rested" on the Sabbath and had outlined strange rules and taboos about eating and drinking certain foods. But he had apparently later changed his mind and permitted people like ourselves to eat almost anything and to drink whatever we liked, providing it was not alcoholic.

From my present point of view the religion of my childhood has its humorous aspects and because it was once *my* religion I may feel privileged to poke a little gentle fun at it. But I am by no means cynical or supercilious about it simply because I have been fortunate enough to have surmounted it. Nor is this apparent outgrowing something for which I can take credit. I have become convinced that the hand of God is in all things and that what we call fortunate chance or circumstance is always the opportunity presented by him for us to grow into his ways and to learn of his nature. Moreover, I am sure that the fact that some of us have widened our horizons and have acquired a deeper insight into his nature is not particularly significant in God's eyes. A little more or less cannot make much difference and certainly we can be no greater or less great in God's regard for having a deeper or less deep understanding of him. It seems to me that what matters is the *direction* of ourselves toward that greater understanding which means the continual deepening and strengthening of faith. I at least have had to struggle for faith against the doubts and superstitions to which a too formal religion can give rise. These doubts and superstitions cannot be maintained in the face of the rationalism of the modern world. But it is the great triumph of Christianity that it is not only rationally and intellectually acceptable but that, as one grows in understanding of it, the mind is liberated from fears and superstitions.

The Mennonites

The adventures of which a boy dreams are largely the physical ones, travel and the exploration of distant lands and strange places. The boy cannot know that in the end the greatest of all adventures are the intellectual and spiritual ones, those in which he travels new avenues of thought, reads unusual and revealing books, and perhaps pursues strange philosophies. He cannot know that sometimes too, in peril of soul, he must travel through dark valleys in which there is so little light that meaning and hope disappear. He becomes lost then and wanders until, almost by accident, he reaches those sunny uplands where the light of God shines happily and makes the journey worthwhile.

One can know of these things only in maturity. The boy may dream of distant places and of daring deeds but as a rule even his physical opportunities for adventure are limited. Certainly mine were. Any boy growing up in one of those bleak little prairie towns around the turn of the century found his physical environment generally limited by the distance a team of horses could travel in a single day. Sunday school picnics to a little lake a few miles away represented geographically about as much of the country that we as children learned to know. After school we might wander into the neighbouring fields to watch the threshing gangs or go down to the creek where we could study the frogs and the hawks and gophers. Sometimes we would even walk as far as "The Old

Mound," a low hill a few miles away which was a glacial hump on the otherwise flat prairie. To a boy with imagination it was a romantic place since it had once been the scene of a battle between opposing tribes of Indians. We would search for arrowheads and pemmican pounders. Once we found a skull and part of an old musket, both of which we carried home with great pride. Children can find romance and adventure anywhere, but I know now that it was as bleak a country physically as it was culturally.

But we had books – at least we had them in my father's household, although I think that my own father had more than anyone else in town. We read a great deal; one winter I read the complete works of Charles Dickens. And because there were not the distractions of such things as television and organized activities we were dependent upon ourselves, and our imaginations and inventiveness were permitted to develop. We invented our own games and toys and we learned trades and skills by watching the blacksmith and the stonemason and the carpenters. We were close to nature, the wind and the weather, the flowers and the stars, and the seasons meant much to us. We all had chores to do, but there also seemed to be a surprising lot of time in which to dream and to be lazy. Moreover, our parents, severe and exacting as they were, and certainly narrow in their religious outlook, loved us and were kind. Except for the presence of the ominous God our childhoods were happy.

I look upon my early religious training as I look upon its background of prairie frontier. Just as the frontier had to give way to our present refinements of civilization, so the crude beliefs based upon fundamentalism had to give way to a freer and more Christian outlook. Today faith can be reinforced and supported by those very factors which in the earlier days were regarded as undermining it. But it was not until much later that I was to know these things and in the meantime I had to go through mental struggle and spiritual distress tinged always with the fears that had been instilled into me as a child.

I have been singularly fortunate in life and I can never understand why. Privileges such as books, education in many fields, travel, good health, financial adequacy, friends and love have undeservedly come my way. Sometimes when I look upon those who have still not found their way from the restrictions of literalism into the higher freedom of God's love, or even worse, when I look upon those who have enclosed themselves within the literalism of scientific laws, I can only say as John Bradford said, "There but for the grace of God go I." The adventure of life is an adventure in freedom, and freedom, I was to learn, must not be circumscribed by rules and laws and regulations and especially not by fears and assumptions which limit the human soul in its explorations. The greatest adventure of all has been the exploration into ultimate reality.

I have never experienced one of those "conversions" which were so common in my younger days at the revival meetings in which the sinner is suddenly saved by fervid admonitions to "Accept Christ as your personal saviour" especially when accompanied by the suggestion, if not by the actual threat, "tomorrow it may be too late." I knew perfectly well as a boy that I was a sinner and according to all my conceptions of sin, I still am, but I had to make my own slow and painful way to a faith in God and the sense of God's forgiveness of sin. I have had flashes of insight into God's love and mercy, but I know nothing of the Damascus Road type of experience in which one suddenly steps from an enclosing framework of thought and action into a new freedom. Those revivalists of my youth who counted the saved by the number who found their way to what was called

"The mercy seat" of the skating rinks in which such affairs were held, may have frightened me but they never drew me closer to God. I am not at all cynical concerning such conversions. Others may have found joy and happiness through them and I have certainly known some changed lives as a result of revival meetings, but I can speak only for myself – they were not for me.

I was to learn that to be free is to have the privilege of making mistakes. In freedom there are always doubts since one must make choices, and the mistakes one makes always carry with them their own unhappy consequences. There have often been long stretches of desolation in my life in which there was a sense of having been deserted by God. Others may have experienced this also and I take some comfort in the thought that in his last moments on the cross Christ experienced it when he cried, "My God, My God, why hast thou forsaken me?" It may be that this sense of separation, this complete alienation from the source of our reality, is the true death of which we become aware from time to time in our lives, and which Christ too had to experience as the wages of sin which he accepted on our account. I was to learn that whether we are aware of it or not we live by love, and if we face moments when we feel that love has been withdrawn, it is because we have permitted ourselves to fall into the isolation of self-love.

Others must have had these same experiences since it is the lot of man. I write about them now since to share them is, I hope, to bring comfort to those who have known them also. I know that we can all give good advice and expound knowledge, and it is certainly a pleasure to share our joys, but I sometimes think that our greatest gift to our fellowman is to share his sorrows. I have found that the feeling of being alone and deserted is one of the hardest things to bear. But if now we learn that there are others who suffer the same distress, the same sense of isolation and incompleteness and meaninglessness and failure, then we can renew our courage and face our trials as being the common lot. But even more when I was to learn eventually that the sense of desolation could extend even to Jesus Christ who was one with us in these matters, then I could renew hope and take courage in the knowledge that through him these evils of the spirit were to be overcome.

But such things were to be discoveries of the future. As a boy, being brought up in the ominous shadow of a punishing God I certainly could have had no idea of how my God concepts would eventually unfold into the Christian God of love. Years were to pass. But first I was to meet new cultural and religious environments which were to make their contributions to my spiritual growth. They were the result of the return of my parents to their Mennonite background in which I was to find a new outlook on religion. Later I was to face the intellectual sophistication of college life in the city.

The Mennonites whom I came to know were, like the Methodists I had left, equally fundamentalist. But unlike the Methodists there was a much calmer acceptance of God and of God's ways. The question of salvation never seemed to arise — it was taken for granted that as a member of the church and of the community of God that God's grace and forgiveness was being extended and received by all. There was at that time none of this, "Repent and be saved – tomorrow it may be too late" frenzy which was later to be brought in by their co-religionists from Kansas and Ohio who by this time had become more or less Americanized and had assimilated much of the sound and fury of the American Bible Belt.

For the Mennonites in those days the Bible was God's word and that was all there was to it. One did not read new meanings into the Bible as is done today or deny that certain accounts therein were not true because they were not within the usual course of events. The Bible was not to be regarded in any way as symbolical – the world was actually created in six twenty-four hour days, the ass which spoke to Balaam spoke in a language which needed no further translation, and Jonah was swallowed by a real and not by a symbolical whale. What was written was written and heaven and earth would pass away before one jot or tittle should be changed. The law was to be fulfilled and no dispute was permissible.

One would think that such rigidity of outlook and belief would make for a corresponding rigidity of judgment whereby God is seen as stern and exacting and ready to visit punishment upon the sinner. But somehow or other I did not feel in this new community that fear played the same authority in my thinking as it had done in the past. One acquires the religious outlook of the community in which one lives, and the religious attitude in this new Mennonite community was much more one of quiet and calm acceptance of God than that to which I had been accustomed. These people, with their literal acceptance of the Bible as being the Word of God were undoubtedly pervaded through and through with beliefs which they regarded as factually true, and must have been subject to what today we would call superstition. But they did not allow their belief in facts to interfere with a Christian faith which apparently did not depend upon doctrines and rationalization. They trusted in the higher wisdom of God to work out any contradictions if indeed they were aware of them.

I was to learn years later that such simple faith which is not harried by rationalizations or dependent upon doctrine is the one actually acceptable to God. Certainly Christ when he healed those who came to him for help, was never concerned as to their structure of beliefs. Jew or Gentile, doctrinally different we may be sure, in faith, were one to him insofar as they trusted in God's goodness and power. And so it was with these unpretentious Mennonite folk. They had a faith beyond the clutter of beliefs, and in many cases they had a serenity of mind which could come only with the assurance that they were under God's care.

I first became aware of this calmness of spirit, this unquestioning faith in God, on attending some of the funerals of the community. I had always been taught to be afraid of death, that it was the greatest of all calamities. But here I was to learn that death, although never welcomed, was not to be dreaded but was simply to be faced with fortitude and accepted as the will of God. Tears and sorrow were always its accompaniment, but there was none of this, "Why should this happen to me?" There was the comforting assurance that those who had gone were now in God's hands and the loss of loved ones by no means destroyed that sense of God's presence and God's peace in which so many of them lived.

Of course there were exceptions as there always are. There were the occasional wild ones and the rebels who defied authority and occasionally there was the downright rotter, but I am speaking here of the general spirit of the community which had an influence over my thinking. Looking back upon it I would say that it was characterized by something which could almost be called a blessedness, and that it differed from the community which I had left in that it did not seem to live under that obsessive shadow of sin. It was as if for these people sin had already been overcome despite the fact that they still had to be alert against its pitfalls and live under its consequences. Christ had died for them and they felt that as long as they held to that belief they were secure. Much of "the peace of God" was actually theirs.

As in the case of my childhood in an all-Canadian town, I could tell a great deal about this all-Mennonite town of my boyhood. It was another prairie town and had an amazing charm. But I am telling in this book about spiritual development, the adventure toward Truth which has made life wonderful and given it a goal. And in this town of my boyhood together with the surrounding villages which were transplanted from Southern Russia, some of my fondest recollections are those concerning the churches and the church services. I liked the Mennonite church services because they had a kind of meditative quality about them which suited my temperament whereas formerly I had regarded church as something one merely sat through for a tiresome hour from a sense of duty.

The ministers in the Mennonite churches were selected from the more devout members of the community and had been nominated by the Elders to preach. After accepting their responsibilities as owing more to God than to the church, they were then ordained by the chief Elder or "Bishop" and henceforth preached at the various churches scattered throughout the countryside without ever being assigned a definite charge. One never knew for certain just who was to preach in the local church that day. As non-professionals, for they were not paid, they had no particular eloquence to display nor, I am sure, any particular sermon to plan. I think they preached largely as the spirit moved them. There were never any loud exhortations or threats of eternal damnation, at least I never heard any, although by the time I was to leave that little town for high school and college in the city, some of the evangelical fervour and calls to repentance were already being brought in via the American school teachers.

The church services, as I said, had a meditative

quality about them which I liked. We drifted into the church and sat down. Then there was a prayer, a hymn, perhaps two, a reading from the Scriptures as the text for the day, followed by a long and sometimes rambling discourse before the final prayer and benediction. It was all very unpretentious; there was no choir, no collection, no standing up and sitting down, no polished sermon like those I was later to hear many times in the city churches. One simply went to church, listened for an hour or so, and came away not so much uplifted as with a happy feeling of having joined in a Christian community and partaken of its fellowship.

Moreover the hymns were lovely. In my former Sunday School days we were continually throwing out the life-line to some poor sinner, or rescuing the perishing, or counting the moments as the clock ticked its ominous message, "Eternity, Where?" to a poor soul dying beyond hope of repentance, or perhaps peeping into a tent where a gypsy boy lay dying. Sometimes too we sang lustily "Beulah Land, Sweet Beulah Land" and "Yes, Jesus loves me" but I cannot recall ever having been spiritually uplifted by them any more than by singing "Twenty froggies went to school" for the second grade teacher. Perhaps I was just too young. But the hymns of the Mennonite churches were those of the Reformation and although I have since heard the voices of the Sistine Choir and those of the Mormon Tabernacle in Salt Lake City and some amazing masses sung by Russian Cathedral Choirs, I still cherish those Sunday morning hymns of my Mennonite days as a gift of my ethnic background. For to hear a hundred or more mixed voices, lacking all self-consciousness as to vocal excellence, some rolling bass and some piercingly shrill, but all amazingly blended into a volume of praise and faith in which individual differences were lost, continuing through twenty or more verses to one of the dignified melodies of Luther's day, is indeed a memory to cherish. All the more perhaps when it is coupled as it often was then with the sound of birds and the smell of new earth and the snow disappearing and the water running and the unhurried greetings and neighborly chatting of the churchgoers as they made their way home or drifted to their teams.

Because the Bible – and no thanks to Luther – had been translated into High German the church services were carried on in that language. It was a Sunday language like the Sunday suit. But in everyday life their conversation and their thinking was done in Low German which, like the French Canadian, is classified as a patois and is still spoken by the old-timers although the new generation is forgetting it. It has a Dutch base and had come down almost unchanged from the days of the Reformation.

I learned it quickly. It is a lovely language, simple and to the point and much like English, differing from that convoluted High German in which I was later to major at college, and from which – I sometimes think by the grace of God – I escaped, since I was once offered a post in the Department of German at the University of Toronto. But I have always felt that the simple, uncluttered language of the Mennonite, so little changed from the early days of their founder, Menno Simon, was singularly appropriate to carry their own uncluttered faith which had also changed so little through one migration after another into the twentieth century. It would almost seem as if the religious outlook was embedded in the language.

Interestingly enough I have just come across an article in a contemporary Mennonite publication which more or less supports this idea. The writer* in discussing a story written in Low German which had

*Menno Wiebe, Mennonite Mirror, November 1973.

appeared in a previous issue, raises what he calls the "theological dimensions" of that language and suggests that it may help us in an appraisal of the earthy aspects of Mennonite theology. "Low German theology," he states, "if we can detect it sufficiently, may in the end be the more honest theology of the Dutch Mennonites than that which has been borrowed from Luther, Calvin, Eduard Wuest, and American evangelicals."

It was that "honest theology" of the Dutch Mennonites to which I was exposed as a growing boy and which, I am sure, has influenced my thinking and my striving since it gave me a sense of the Peace of God which so many in that community seemed to have reached. Of those other influences mentioned, borrowed from Luther and Calvin and others, I knew nothing except perhaps those of the American evangelicals who, even in the short ten years or so in which I was to live among them, were beginning to infect the calm faith of the Mennonite community with problems of guilt and sin and hell and punishment and, of course, the imminent Second Coming of the Lord at which occasion all nations were to be judged according to the Great Plan.

I have never formally belonged to the Mennonite Church and have not lived among them for many years. They have changed greatly since my day, naturally so, since the first generation of pioneers to which I seem tenuously to still belong, has since been replaced by new generations who have been exposed to our modern age. Many of the virtues attendant upon the simple faith of their fathers have fallen away. Assimilation into the Canadian culture and economy, industrialization, education and prosperity – above all prosperity – have presented temptations and problems unknown to the early first immigrants. That the change has not always been for the better is not surprising. But in my own mind I blame a great deal upon the imported Evangelicals who, more than any Luther or Calvin would have done, were even in my time beginning to taint the Mennonite theology. They were assiduous, diligent, hard working, and urgent. They were busy earning God's love instead of accepting it.

Some of these evangelicals were a combination of British-Israelite and Jehovah Witness as well as being exhorters. I recall in particular one earnest soul from Ohio, one of my teachers in fact, who in a series of weekly evening talks outlined all of God's plans for the future. He would unfold long charts and illustrations to prove his points and our young minds were much impressed especially with the pictures of a seven-headed dragon or of some monster with feet of iron and head of brass – I am no longer sure of his metallic composition – who was to be thrown into a lake of fire after the prescribed time had expired. Numerology seemed to enter into it also; as I recall it the number seven had some particular significance and the years involved were in terms of a thousand or several thousands, I forget which.

Now I have no objections to speculations based on the apocryphal Books of the Bible and it is certainly not for me to dispute them since for all I know they may be true or not true. I can also read the Book of Revelation with interest especially in the King James version for its language and imagery, but just what John's vision on the Isle of Patmos is all about I have not the faintest idea at least not in any specific sense. To me it is simply the work of some great writer, who, like the author of the Book of Job, was of outstanding talent and poetic inspiration. In The Revelation he is pouring forth his faith and his conviction in the ultimate triumph of God addressed especially to the Jewish converts to Christ since, in the Jewish hopes, the coming of the Messiah, the Great Day of the Lord, was always linked up with the overcoming of their historical enemies.

Be that as it may I can only speak of my reactions to what I now regard as perverted evangelical teaching. This was to be my problem. Not merely God. Not the existence of God, and the recognition of his creative power, but the kind of God – his nature, his character, his purpose. That was to be the search, the adventure, the doubts.

College Days

I don't think that my college days as such were very fruitful from the standpoint of spiritual growth. I was learning a great deal academically and developing intellectually but as I recall my twelve years or so at three different universities, I cannot say that I acquired anything in the way of wisdom. I seem to have had brains enough to worry my way, and in some cases even bluff my way, through the various courses, but I never faced those basic problems of life which I was to meet later and which were to cause me so much of doubt and distress. The First World War and the later influenza epidemic were realities which raised questions of survival rather than those of life's meaning and destiny. What the war and the epidemic confronted us with was the fact of death but college life and college learning contributed nothing to its understanding.

I set no great store by learning. I can admire it as I can admire skill, but even the most skillful craftsman or the artist who is master of all the tools and technique of his art, can accomplish nothing of worth without inner greatness. And that we lacked as students. Students are great thinkers but they think to no great purpose. The meaning of life, of love, of guilt, the tragedy of death, the problem of evil, the nature of God, such things could be discussed academically but because they did not enter into our lives as realities they received little more than the academic treatment. We were shallow, half-baked, and we thought as students still do, that we knew it all.

I had always wanted to go to college. Even as a boy I was very much the philosopher and used to meditate on the nature of space and time and the meaning of such abstractions as eternity and infinity. I remember explaining to one of the boys in my class in elementary school the inevitability of the passing of time, and I kicked a clod and explained that that was a single event which had happened and could never happen again regardless of how many clods I kicked. Also I had a very strong sense of my own identity as an individual, and I still remember the surprising realization as a little boy which came to me one afternoon of being a person in my own right apart from other persons and that my consciousness was actually self-consciousness apart from theirs. These are philosophically profound ideas as I was to discover much later and I have made much use of them in my philosophical thinking, but my college courses in formal philosophy threw little light upon such concepts. It was not until I learned that God was not only the existing God of the philosophers but also the loving God of humanity that I began to understand them.

Any boy who reflects upon the "beginning" of time or asks himself what lies in space "beyond the utmost bounds of human thought," or who, even as a child, asks his mother, "Who made God?" is already a philosopher and most children are. They have not always had my opportunities for pursuing their questions formally. But in my case I was plagued with an inherited tendency to inquire into all things as well as to raise many doubts concerning all things, so that I drifted into philosophy at the university as a matter of course. My mother's younger brother whom we all regarded as very educated and intelligent had graduated in Philosophy Honours at the University of Manitoba before taking a degree in Medicine at McGill and I felt I should emulate him. But quite apart from that, I had the idea that philosophy would enlighten me in the whys and wherefores of all things and I would then know the secrets of the universe. But alas, the dreams of youth! I satisfied my desires only to say with Omar:

> My self, when young, did eagerly frequent,
> Doctor and Saint, and heard great argument,
> About it and about: but evermore
> Came out by the same door wherein I went.

The Honours course in Philosophy and even an extra year post-graduate work in that subject at another university left me completely disillusioned. After five years of study, I knew even less than I had known before concerning the nature and secrets and meaning of life. Being always dubious as to the validity of most of the theories presented to us as students I certainly never distinguished myself in any of the courses. The students in Theology who took these courses with me always carried off the prizes at examination time. My trouble seems to have been, as one of my professors once told me: "You take a philosophical idea and you pry it apart and then drop a nut into it." The side courses such as ethics, aesthetics, psychology, and sociology I found interesting enough but the actual substance of philosophy which is supposed to penetrate into ultimates and first causes and prime movers I was to find exceedingly disappointing.

I undoubtedly learned the technique of examining critically the different methods of thought, a technique which has stood me in good stead in dealing with the materialistic philosophies of today and in finding basic fallacies. But as far as my actual knowledge was concerned the whole problem of meaning was now merely more confused and complicated, certainly I was not more enlightened. In fact the whole of college life, though it gave me much more material to work with than I had hitherto known revealed no simplifying principle.

We students as self-appointed intellectuals could always toss ideas around and we had frequent discussions in which we would take the universe apart without putting it together again. Like the youth of today we were rebels and like the youth of today we had many remedies to suggest how the world could be made perfect for humanity. These in the end amounted to the same suggestions which are being advanced today by all politicians and social reformers and forward-lookers to the effect that if only everybody would be good then everything would be good. We, like they, overlooked the deep-seated sin in human nature which does not respond to calls for social reform. Moreover as students unconcerned with God, we could hardly have had any sense of sin. That, in my case, was to come later when I began to reflect more and more on the nature of God and especially on God's lovingness as revealed through Christ.

Although we had no particular sense of purpose or destiny we were not on that account rebels against religion. We generally belonged to the Y.M.C.A., which although not particularly Christian, was full of synthetic good-fellowship and emphasized sexual morality and citizenship and "clean living." We attended the most popular of the city churches and heard eloquent and fluent sermons in favour of social advancement which were much after the manner of a good Board of Trade pep talk. Christ was the great humanitarian, a man who had the welfare of his fellowmen at heart. The choirs and quartets in these fashionable churches were beautifully trained and their splendid voices were as much an inducement to attend the Sunday evening services as were the intellectual sermons themselves.

Sometimes, more or less out of curiosity, we would

go slumming into the more emotional sects at out of the way churches where groans and shouts and sometimes even writhing on the floor proclaimed "the presence of the spirit" according to one of my language instructors in German who was in charge. But a visiting team of revivalists was also still considered a good show, for it brought back memories of the days of my childhood. Once when I was a student in Toronto I even took a train to Buffalo to hear the famous Billy Sunday who in an arena the size of a soccer field was nightly turning his thousands to repentance. I had heard much about this celebrity and "hit the sawdust trail," which was his slogan for repentance. In order to get a closeup view of the famous man and receive his "God bless you" I filed past the improvised altar in which a deep notch had been cut so that he could reach down and shake the hands of the penitents. To my young male mind his vivid description of Salome's dance before Herod together with details of her costume or rather her lack of costume "She came in with one leg at a quarter to twelve and she didn't wear enough to flag a hand-car" was particularly intriguing, but as in the case of the fashionable city churches there was little spiritual food.

Looking back, I cannot say that during my student days I ever really asked for the bread of life. Being a reasonably bright student I was satisfied to learn about such things as Ultimates and Universals in philosophical terms without making any personal commitment which I was to discover was necessary for true knowledge concerning them. God was simply one of the metaphysical factors, or perhaps according to some, *the* sole metaphysical fact in all reality. But he made no demands upon us. There was nothing there concerning which one could say with conviction, "This will I accept and according to this will I live." At least I was beginning to learn in a negative way that a philosophy which lacks the vital element of purpose is sterile.

My personal friends at college were invariably Jews, at least Jews were the companions with whom I associated most. I liked them because they were clever, original, and brought to all things a light cynicism and non-acceptance which was in accord with my own inherited temperament, that of unbelief. Not that I did not believe in God. I believed in him enough to pray to him at night as I had been taught to do. I was also in one respect a Christian in that I believed in Christ as one who acted as mediator between me and God in the matter of my sins, but actually I was not very conscious of sins either. I did not drink, I did not steal, I did not seduce my girl friends, in fact I did not descend to the "baser" sins against which I had been warned by my mother and my early training in Sunday School. But I was not on that account self-righteous. I had long ago outgrown those little prohibitions which were once considered violations of God's laws, such as doing homework on the Sabbath or having a congenial game of poker with my friends, or being strongly addicted to a foul pipe. Such departures from the once-prohibited behaviour did not make me feel sinful any more than the abstinence from the "baser" sins gave me any sense of virtue. Perhaps by this time I was already growing into a higher concept of God as one who was not so piffling as to make arbitrary demands upon my conduct as I had been taught to believe. I was eventually to become very aware of the meaning of sin and to suffer greatly from a sense of guilt, but this was to come later in life and not during those comparitively carefree college days.

But if formal education, Philosophy and another major course in German literature, were to contribute little to my spiritual growth, the First World War, that sudden catastrophe in history was to bring me face to face with reality, especially the fact and problem of death. It was that First World War which brought the placid and self-satisfied Victorian age to its close. It was a war which as far as I was concerned and despite all the slogans and patriotic speeches and posters and parades, smelled of death. At least half of my classmates never returned from the trenches in Flanders.

I had been brought up in the Mennonite tradition whose main tenet of belief is pacifism. I suppose I used this training to rationalize my disinclination to enlist. Pacifism certainly does not make for physical courage, moreover I had been brought up to fear death and the judgment of God. "It is appointed unto man once to die, but after this is the judgment" from the book of Hebrews was something I had heard again and again throughout my youth. Moreover I was already too much the student of history to believe that the world could be, as they said in those days, "made safe for democracy" by force of arms. Such high-flown slogans I knew had in one form and another characterized every war in history and I believed strongly, as I still do in the Biblical injunction that we should not do evil that good may come of it.

I was too independent a thinker to be moved by the social pressure which was being brought to bear upon my class-mates, but I felt myself to be an alien and an outcast. I had then, and I will always have, a tremendous respect and admiration for those who had the courage and conviction to venture their lives for what they regarded as ideals and freedom. But I could not personally bring myself to do it though I was often tempted more from a sense of loyalty and belonging, than from any conviction. I suppose if I had been conscripted I would have gone to war with resignation and regarded myself as one of the unfortunate victims of history. But I thought then, as I still think, that to defend a social system or a living standard, "blueberry pie" as the Americans used to call it in those days, was not a justifiable reason for killing or permitting myself to be killed by my fellow-men. I was certainly never pacifist enough to believe that one should abjectly surrender to evil; I would have fought to the death to save and protect someone I loved, but to lay down my life for what I regarded as material considerations, especially after having listened to a great deal of talk about this being a "Capitalists' war," struck me as particularly futile. To make sacrifices, in fact to have courage, one must have conviction and faith. These I lacked.

I have often asked myself in the course of years whether my actions were right or wrong in the matter of that first war. Those boys who were enlisting day after day were my fellow students and my personal friends and I wanted to belong. But this I also know, that if I had accepted some of the safe and cushy jobs which had been offered to me because of my educational advantages and my later positon as a newsman on the daily paper and had then made a pretense of supporting the war without a sense of conviction in the matter, I would have felt myself to be a "slacker" and a wearer of the white feather. As it was, I may have been apologetic but I was not ashamed, and in my thoughts at least I faced up to the firing squad if it were to come to that. Whether or not my courage would have stood up in the end I do not know. But that which finally put the cap on all my wavering doubts and resolutions was something which had been said by a Church of England priest: "I cannot see Christ behind a machine gun."

Having escaped the war I was still to face death personally in the great flu epidemic which followed. I was very ill for many weeks and my brothers told me later that they had all expected me to die. But in the end I recovered and I think it was because of the personal reality of God. I prayed to him a great deal during those anxious days, not, for once, because of fear, but because I wanted my life to be prolonged so that it might become something worth while. I had become very much aware that my life had so far been trivial and fruitless.

I am very convinced that it was God who sustained me and helped me back to health. I know that the pure scientist and the mechanist will never agree and will say that I would have recovered in any case. But faith and love and hope can never be evaluated in scientific terms and one does not pray without them. We do not know just how God acts in our lives, and even if we were to say that such things as faith and hope are psychological elixirs which help us overcome illness, they are merely being given names. They still emanate from God who is the source of all life.

Death is the denial of life, its final indignity. We shun it and avoid it and yet I often wonder what we as human beings would spiritually become if there was no such fact as death. I know that to some who are in pain and sorrow it can come as a blessed relief and I know that there are many like myself who look to a new life in God. But in the normal course of affairs when we are concerned with living, growing, adventuring, enjoying, loving, then death when it comes is the most tragic of events. It seems to put the seal of annihilation upon life itself, and regardless of any of our scientific rationalizations as to its social and biological necessity and all that, it erases all meaning if we see it in terms of finality. Fame, fortune, power, our treasured acquisitions, even our treasured friends and those we love, all, all become meaningless incidents in the great flow of time if time itself is ended by the event of death.

Such is the stark, brutal fact of death from which we are rescued only by the Christian faith. Whatever one may think of Christ and of Christianity as a religion, it makes that one tremendous assertion that in the end life triumphs over death and that life's meaning is not destroyed by death. There are other religions, of course, some very old, which cling to the belief in an immortality of sorts, an immortality in which the soul wanders in a kind of shadow world, or in the course of transmigration finds its way into other organisms, or even drifts finally into some great consciousness in which its personal identity is lost. But in comparison with all these, Christianity simply soars. It not only states that each personal life with its own private identity shall live again, but that its means of communication, its expression, what we here call "the flesh", shall be restored, and that with it those baser meanings which we have acquired in life shall fall away so that life may be more abundant.

It took me a long time to realize finally that in this wonderfully planned world we must have death as a necessity for our final creation. We are all more or less lost in self-involvement which is an alienation from God as well as from others. We would drift endlessly into an alone-ness of self if death did not intervene. The Apostle Paul understood this: "Unless a grain of wheat falls into the earth and dies, it remains alone," and to be completely alone means that all those outward-extending qualities of the human dynamic such as love and hope fall back upon themselves. We know that the process of ingrowingness can to some extent be reversed by the love for others and for God. But since in the very gift of our human-ness we are all born into the sin of self-involvement, we must all die. And I ask myself how we could ever know anything about God and about the ultimate nature of love unless he were to rescue us from ourselves by the fact of death.

It seems that St. Paul received a quick knowledge of the truth concerning death in that sudden flash of revelation on the Damascus Road. To others less gifted, the acquiring of such knowledge is often long and painful. It was certainly long and painful in my own case, for it meant casting aside old fears and superstitions and certainly the old beliefs upon which such fears were based, and in the process of discarding them leaving empty areas which seemed all the more spiritually desolate because they were empty. That alone-ness of spirit which accompanies doubt is in itself a foretaste of death because spiritual doubts are never an acceptance of some other belief but a condition in which the human spirit is poised on a kind of brink of desolation and despair. Doubts concerning God are not, as doubts in science, the weighing of evidence before choosing that which is regarded as being more rationally acceptable. Doubts concerning God involve us as persons, and because as persons we cannot completely commit ourselves into God's hands, we suffer as persons. The Castles of doubt we build ourselves are indeed often occupied by a giant called Despair.

The Contributions of Science

My college days were over. True, I was later to go back to the universities but with a different purpose and a different attitude of mind. The war had matured us all and in any case youth was on the way out. That easygoing, unconcerned, and generally thoughtless transition period from boyhood into manhood which are called student days are generally considered to be happy since they involve no particular responsibility beyond passing examinations. Moreover in those days the universities were much more human institutions compared with the computerized mills of today with their efficiencies and quantitative scale of values. Persons counted more than degrees; one entered a community of educated men and by something resembling osmotic pressure acquired a cultural outlook together with the specialized education whereby one was admitted to the intellectually elite. They may have been very much ivory towers but they were delightful towers in which originality and even eccentricities were taken for granted. Academic freedom in those days meant tolerance of mind and receptivity to ideas and not as now a constitutional right. I would have liked to have stayed on as a student but I now had my living to make and was faced with the problem of what to do with my life.

I tried various things. A summer in journalism decided me against it as being just too trivial. What I wrote today was forgotten tomorrow, and rightly so.

My real trouble was that by now I had a vague feeling that I must not just make use of my talents and abilities for my own private advantage but that life to be satisfying had to be lived within a sense of worth. That is why I also abandoned the study of law after being articled as a law student for one summer. I liked it very much and I found, probably because of my training in philosophy that I was very good at it. But again it was not spiritually satisfying. I could see myself as a successful man of law, perhaps eventually a judge, but some submerged conscience deep in my religious background seemed to prevent me from giving myself to it whole-heartedly.

Teaching and medicine suggested themselves. I had always edged away from the thought of becoming a medical doctor because I hated any contact with disease and pain, but I finally decided it was my duty to take a course in medicine. In the meantime I had to make some money, so I took one of the quick courses in education which were available in those days, a trivial, pretentious affair but which gave me a professional standing and enabled me to teach in the schools of Manitoba. I was quite happy to be a teacher and after being principal of two schools it might well have become my life's work if the opportunity had not suddenly presented itself to teach in the university.

I was offered a very minor job in the Chemistry Department at the University of Manitoba which came about because the year before, in anticipation of my entering the Medical College, I had returned to the University to take the necessary sciences without which I would not have been permitted to enter. Apparently, I had impressed my professors as having ability in science, and in addition I was by now older than the students I was called upon to teach and I had a post-graduate degree from Toronto as well as the one in Arts from Manitoba. The opportunity to return to the pleasant university life was too tempting to resist so I resigned my school and a month later was on the way to becoming a scientist and eventually a professor of chemistry.

I would have much preferred to have been teaching philosophy for which I was temperamentally and academically qualified, but there were no openings available. I wanted above all to be a teacher and it did not greatly matter to me just what I taught. There was the personally gratifying feeling of doing something for others while making a congenial and more or less comfortable living at the same time.

I was not ambitious. Life, I felt, should be savoured and not eroded by any great pursuit of success. I would have been quite content to have remained a country school teacher but it presented complications. In those days all the parents in the rural community seemed to take turns in finding fault with the teacher – his church attendance, his probable atheism because he was a university graduate, his weekend visits to the city, his walks along the river after school with the junior room teacher, his childishness in showing some of the boys in his class on Saturday how to make and fly a box kite, his severity in maintaining discipline, his lack of severity in maintaining discipline, his this, his that. Such things never bothered me greatly – I had been brought up in the little towns and had learned to take them with a grain or more of salt. The problems of discipline among high school boys who tend at that age to be rebels, and the problem of keeping some of the charming high school girls at arm's length, literally, who tended to acquire a "crush" on a young, unmarried, and reasonably pleasant teacher, were not problems to be faced at the university. Moreover the university, apart from the fact that I was spiritually at home there, had the overwhelming advantage of being in session only eight months of the year instead of ten. I loved long holidays.

In this vaguely reminiscent and autobiographical book I find myself referring to "those days", but those days are significant only insofar as they affected my progress in the search for the unchanging God. And I think that my scientific years are particularly significant in that through the study and teaching of science I was able to resolve some of the problems which had always plagued me as to how God acted in the material world. I could not accept him in my heart while my mind rejected him. I felt that to blindly "believe!" as I had once been taught to do involved me in superstitions and fear. I felt that the Christian injunction to love the Lord our God with all our heart and soul *and mind* was still very valid since the ability to reason and rationalize was also a gift from him. The difficulty was that the great separation between the apparently unconcerned world of matter and energy in which we live, and the supposedly very much personally concerned world of the spirit in which God was supposed to live always stood in the way.

In the matter of religion, the material world was believed to have been God's creation, yet there appeared to be precious little of God in it. It seemed to work impersonally and mechanically and with complete indifference as far as man's good or bad was concerned. The conclusion which seemed to be forced upon me was either that God, having created the world in the first place, had then completely withdrawn from it leaving it to its own mechanical devices, or perhaps that there was no God involved in it at all. The acceptance of the world as being a purely mechanical system without God was then, as now, the scientific point of view as it still is that of modern scientific intellectualism which has grown out of science.

I have already dealt in detail with the scientific assumption of a mechanical universe in a previous book called "Tower in Siloam." I pointed out in this book that once God, regarded as a Personal reality underlying all things, is denied, then human thought must of necessity fall into the mechanical mould in its rationalizations. It must regard all things as falling within a system of impersonal, that is, mechanical, or scientific laws. There is no choice in the matter. We must either think of the material universe as being within the mind and purpose of a personal God, or as not being within any mind and purpose whatsoever which is materialism. In analysing the method of scientific thought in the matter of its explanations for the events and objects of this universe, I pointed out that scientific thought in its so-called explanations, is not only unsound but philosophically shallow. It takes observed generalizations and calls them laws and then offers these laws as causes to account for the events. In fact the whole system of causality in scientific thinking rests upon laws and the "forces" which are said to abide within the laws. It is because these causal forces are regarded as impersonal that they are a denial of God. Moreover science denies that there is any permanent reality. It states that all structures sooner or later disintegrate and disappear. This generalization, also called a law, is the very basic "Law of Maximum Entropy". What it means in layman's language is that the energy of our universe, insofar as we know it, is running out. The cosmic clock is unwinding.

I noticed however that science cannot give any explanation for the cosmic clock having been wound in the first place. The *origin* of all the spatial and energy structures which constitute our material universe are a deep mystery to scientific thought since on its assumption of impersonal causes it can only describe *what* brought them into being, and never *Who* created them or *why*. Lacking the concept of

Personality as a factor in its thinking it can see no purpose in the whole physical world or in the living organic world which is presumed to have evolved from it. In the last analysis its explanations rest upon the no-cause, "probability" which is the scientific way of saying that it's all just a matter of luck.

Because of this inadequacy in scientific thinking I was coming to realize that problems concerning origins and causes are not really scientific but philosophical and religious. Unthinking people, particularly those who are wishfully unthinking in refuting God, readily adopt the scientific point of view. In my own case, having never abandoned the belief in God, my difficulty lay in reconciling the hard, tangible, scientific world of experience, that of "the flesh" as it was known in my Sunday School days, with that rarified off-by-itself world of the spirit which was not subject to the pains and anxieties and sorrows of the one in which we live. "Flesh and blood," I had been taught, "cannot inherit the Kingdom of God." And thus the difference between them was emphasized.

I was to learn eventually that the so-called flesh, by which is meant the whole material world of which our bodies are a part, is actually the dynamic expression of the spirit and that there is no real dividing line between the two aspects of reality. But I certainly did not learn this until I had finished my formal scientific training, although I was very fortunate in having professors in both physics and chemistry who had fine minds and would occasionally during lectures in an almost casual aside open up a whole field for later speculation. As it was, it was not until I had taught science for a number of years that I began to have some understanding of the underlying nature of what I was teaching.

I think it was because I always felt that in teaching one of the physical sciences I was a square peg in a round hole that I tended to reflect more upon the religious and philosophical implications of the subject which I was teaching than did any of my more brilliant colleagues. The truth is that I was not a good scientist. I had fallen into the teaching of it more or less by accident against my temperamental inclinations, and although I was good enough to put myself through the various years of training and research by fellowships and scholarships, actually to me it was all just a job without my ever having in it a consuming interest. I certainly lacked that quick, steel-trap mind which a good physical scientist is supposed to have which can seize upon physical relationships and express them in the quantitative language of mathematics.

But I was a good teacher. A teacher I had always wanted to be and although the physical sciences are cold and impersonal, in the matter of teaching them the scene can be shifted to a human relationship in which personality reaches out to personality. I sometimes used to wonder, even in the middle of one of my lectures, as to just what on earth I was actually doing in this process of teaching. Here am I, I would tell myself, and there, apart from me in the lecture theatre, are they, the students. And between us something quite astonishing is happening. From the purely scientific point of view I am sending them sound waves which are of different structure and complexity. From their point of view these structures are more than physical waves, they are symbols carrying meanings. What I was doing was actuating the physical system between us, in this case the air, in such a manner as to establish a meaningful communication between person and persons.

It was a sharing process. It was a sharing of knowledge which in this case happened to be mine and which they were willing to receive. But the *willingness* to receive was something personal which, to be a good teacher, I also had to establish. I had to break down barriers which persons continually build against knowledge and against each other. The human mind is not just a slate on which knowledge is written; it must reach out toward the source of knowledge and I felt that in teaching I had to establish a rapport between myself and students so that personality could respond to personality. It is a dynamic situation, a process in which giving and receiving is always to some extent mutual. Certainly I felt that these young minds, reaching out toward me and *trusting* me to have greater knowledge and to guide them in their course, were at the same time enriching my own life and giving me a knowledge. I know too that from these reflections I have learned a great deal concerning the relationship between myself and God, knowledge concerning the symbolical structures carrying meaning, knowledge concerning trust and the willingness to receive.

I was a good teacher for another reason. Although I knew my subject matter I was not at heart a scientist and for that reason I found much of the complex scientific relationships difficult to follow. I often had to work hard and long for my own understanding of them and therefore I had a sympathetic attitude toward my students concerning these difficulties. I could be patient and lucid, whereas I had learned from my own experience as a student, the more able scientist tended to fire information on the assumption that because it was obvious to him it must be equally obvious to those he was teaching. I sometimes think that one of the qualifications of a good teacher is that he not be particularly clever. This, I was to learn in the course of my professorship, was the case with most of those graduates who later took education and became excellent teachers in the schools.

I am always very thankful for having been trained in the physical sciences and in having to teach them as subjects for which I was temperamentally unfitted. Naturally as a scientist, I was not a success. Despite the fact that I had to some extent distinguished myself in research, the thought of spending further long hours in discovering some hitherto undiscovered factual scientific truth bored me.Moreover one quickly becomes disillusioned as to the nature of the so-called "research" which is carried on in the universities as being trivial and pretentious and I could not feel that by devoting myself to it, I was spending my life within that sense of worth which I felt it must have to be properly lived. The very fact that I was that square peg in a round hole however stood me in good stead, for in reacting against the superficiality of formal science I tended more and more to inquire into the hidden mysteries of the physical world underlying its superficialities.

The factual truths of science, the observed phenomena to be measured and related and tabulated tells us *how* the physical system works. But I found that my concern was no longer how it worked but *why* it should work at all. I was reflecting more and more on the nature of the scientific causes which science calls "force" or forces, and why indeed there should be those regularities within the system which science calls "laws" and whether we could account for ourselves and our complex environment by reference to these laws and forces, and especially to that no-cause which was continually being dragged into scientific explanations under the name of "probability." What I found myself to be doing was applying my philosophical training to a field where it presumably had no business to be, since science can function as science only on the assumption that it is dealing with a mechanical system where such questions as to *why* things act as they do are not permitted because purposiveness and consequently personality would thereby be introduced.

There are, of course, many scientists who recognize the pragmatic necessity for science to accept the idea that nature and the natural world is governed by impersonal laws but they are not themselves content to accept such an impersonal description as explaining its origin and its continuance. In my time there were men like Jeans and Eddington and Whitehead and DuNuöy who were scientific philosophers and who saw behind the surface reality of the material world a greater Reality having mind and plan and purpose. But they did not necessarily see this underlying Reality as what we call God. The tendency among scientific philosophers is to diffuse the concept of God into a principle rather than a Person, but I personally found this unsatisfactory because in my own private philosophy of science I felt the necessity for a very real personal God, particularly I suppose, because I was very aware of my own self as having personal reality.

I read the scientific philosophers with great interest and they have helped me greatly in finally integrating into a coherent rationale those opposing systems of thought within me, namely, religion, philosophy, and science. The one who helped me most was Arthur Eddington with his exposition of the material universe as consisting of "symbolic structures" in which some dynamic principle underlying what we call matter and energy takes on form or structure in such a way that we accept these "action structures" as carrying meaning within themselves. These structures constitute the objective world of matter and energy although they are themselves not material in the usually accepted sense. They are, on a higher level, the same as those structures which we call sound-waves which we send to each other as symbols which carry meaning within them because we have imparted meaning into them. Written words are also symbolic structures which are used for communication between person and person as are also such modification of light-waves whereby we communicate in gestures and smiles, or for that matter such energy waves as are employed in physical contact.

The further consideration of this fact of communication between person and person is very fascinating but I have dealt with it at length in *Tower In Siloam.* One might argue here that the acceptance of such symbolical structures, each carrying its own inherent meaning is, in all logic, already an acceptance of God of sorts, since any meaning inherent in the structures implies that meaning must have been imparted to them from some source in which meaning abides and from which it can emanate. Obviously this source must be personal since an impersonal, or mechanical system, can carry no meaning beyond that which we ourselves read into it.

I did not need science and the scientific philosophers to convince me of the existence of a personal God — my early religious training had seen to that. My interest here was the problem of all philosophers, that of bridging the gap between the material world and the spiritual one, the Flesh and the Word. And now this new "action principle" which science had discovered and into which all things had been reduced, suddenly provided me with the clue whereby the two worlds became one. I suddenly realized that if our whole physical world is composed of "action" structures, thus replacing the old concept of matter and energy existing in space and time, then this discovered "action" must be the very power which personality in its own nature must have in order to express itself, or, to put it another way, in order to communicate.

Now it seemed evident to me that we as persons have this activity principle at our disposal when we *activate* our vocal chords in such a way as to give rise to those meaningful sound structures. It is our will which initiates the action according to whatever plan or purpose we have in mind. And it is evident that if God is a Person, which is to say that he is a Being in whom those vague and indefinable terms associated with personality have become centred and integrated, that he must also have at his disposal the same power to express His will as we do and he must do so in the structural or objective terms with which we are familiar. Certainly Personality existing in a vacuum without the means of expression is meaningless since it can never be known. If there is a God at all he must find his expression. He must communicate. He must reveal Himself. How? Only by his actions, and through this power to act he has created the entire physical universe. It is composed of structures, and it is our great privilege as persons to read these structures in such a way as to see and understand the purposes within them and thereby the will and nature of God himself. What all this means is simply a kind of roundabout way of saying what we have all been taught, that God is creator of this world and that "all things were made by him and without him was not anything made that was made."

The Religious Implications of Science

Having grown up in a churchy environment which was much given over to religious dispute and having also been blessed with an abundance of relatives willing to argue at any moment some of the fine points of religious doctrine, I had already learned that no amount of argument or dispute ever brought one closer to God. As a boy I had listened attentively to such earnest discussions as to whether salvation was "by faith or by works" and as to whether a man who for years had led a "good" life would receive any benefit in the credit column of God's books if he later fell into evil ways. In that early religion of my childhood it appeared that justice and equity were much more important in God's nature than his love.

However in the more sophisticated atmosphere of the halls of learning the religious discussions, when they occurred at all, were generally on a more rarified level involving not so much questions concerning God's nature as to his actual existence. I used to work occasionally in the Students Christian Movements which all colleges still have and I was to find here that the emphasis was generally that of bringing the belief in God, such as it was, in line with modern thought. "Relevance" had to a great extent become the catchword, and the older ideas of personal salvation were being replaced by social good. Christ the Reformer was taking the place of Christ the Redeemer in the minds of the students and a rather nebulous philosophy of humanism was taking over the spiritual house once occupied by beliefs and the sense of personal relationship toward God. Many beliefs had been abandoned in the face of intellectualism and particularly in the face of that modern scientific intellectualism which derides the faith in a personal God as being superstition and intellectually undignified.

No one is immune from the modern attack. There were many, of course, who would have been happy to find a scientific or philosophical proof of God for the sake of having an intellectual sanction for their still lingering faith. Others, like myself, who believed in God, were trying to reconcile the world of spirit with the world of their material existence, and especially to reconcile the God of goodness with the physical world in which there seemed to be so little goodness. They have been called "wistful agnostics", willing to commit themselves to God in their thinking but not quite able to do so. They were plagued by doubts concerning God's goodness and suffered real fear at the thought of falling into that abyss of meaninglessness and personal frustration which would follow the denial of God and God's purposes in human affairs.

I was to decide eventually that the reason there is no scientific or philosophical proof for the existence of God is that it is God himself who supplies the terms in which proof is framed and that there is no system of logic or evidence beyond him into which he can be explained. I did not realize this until I had enlarged more fully that startling concept which the study of science had given me, that the world with all its terms, the entire creation in fact, is composed of that "activity" which I have just mentioned.

I do not know to what extent this identification of an active principle underlying the material world, its "sub-substance" as it were, with the activity of a personal God had already been considered in philosophic thought but to me at least it came as a tremendous discovery. St. John's "In the beginning was the Word, and the Word was with God . . . all things were made by him and without him was not anything made that was made" suddenly found its scientific justification. It was not that science was verifying God – it was that with the acceptance of God as a Personal Being the scientific world had suddenly become explicable.

In a way I have had to argue my own self into the acceptance of God. My faith had always been flawed by doubts. But with this new insight that the substratum of the material world was also the creative activity of God, I was now able to overcome many of the doubts which had stood in the way of complete belief. It would now seem as if a new vista for the mind to explore had been opened for me.

For one thing, the question of the miracles of Christ had always bothered me. Also that cornerstone of the Christian faith, the resurrection of Christ after his crucifixion, together with such associated miracles as his virgin birth had never actually been denied by me but from time to time they had become suspect. But no more. Once the logical connection between God and all the material objects and events of history had been revealed, I could now say to myself with perfect assurance that if God had devised the physical laws underlying those events then there was nothing, but nothing, to prevent him from entering the physical system at any time. If on some occasion he had a special purpose in mind the so-called laws of the physical system would not prevent him from bringing about new events. After all, the natural laws had not been devised for God himself to obey, but for the sake of man so that he would find himself in a sane and rational and dependable environment whereby his own will would be free to act. Although created in the image of God, he had not been given the power to suspend the laws of natural causality and thus perform the miracles which God was able to do. If now Christ was to appear as the God in Man, the Word made Flesh as an actual person, then that person would not be subject to the natural laws of causality even though as a person who identified himself with man he was quite willing to submit to them.

So also with the question of the virgin birth of Christ, another stumbling block to belief which I have heard denied again and again even by ministers of the Gospel who were otherwise quite willing to accept the greater miracle of the resurrection but who regarded any suggestion of immaculate conception as making just too great demands upon human credulity. Perhaps it is because it is not a very important point that it was being discounted although some may not regard it as such; one of my students for example related to me the outcome of an argument concerning it by two other students which ended with them slugging it out on the campus. Just what doctrinal decision was finally reached by this method he was unable to say. However, as far as I was concerned I could now understand that there could be no objection to God entering the causal system of natural events and bringing about a *new* event which would not otherwise have happened in their natural course. Certainly Christ was a *new* man in human history. For this reason it seemed to me to be a logical and necessary act for God to *enter* history at a certain point. My faith in Christ, as well as my intelligence, is strengthened by the belief in the virgin birth.

Another problem which had concerned me greatly in a nagging, uncomfortable way was that of God's ability to enter the physical system in answer to our prayers. God's answers to prayer in personal life so often seems to be such a casual and natural matter that one is inclined to overlook God or to deny him entirely. For example one can say about illness as so many do, that recovery in answer to prayer would have come about anyway, prayer or no prayer. I do not believe this. Those casual and natural matters, the life forces which lead or do not lead to recovery in illness can be tilted in our favour at any time by God since they came from him in the first place. Whether prayers are always answered according to *our* private wishes is another matter entirely. I certainly believe that God not only knows our physical troubles but can reach into the physical system to which we are subject and bring about events which assist us. They are not brought about, at least not in my experience, by that startling and miraculous manner in which they were brought about by Christ. We are faced with a different set of conditions from when God was appearing in person upon the historical scene. But so often in my own life when in distress and even in despair, my appeals to God have been answered in a manner which many would argue is a matter of coincidence. But for me what matters is the fact that my prayers were actually answered and not ignored. The so-called coincidence *did* happen, and by the sheer luck to which it could be attributed it might equally well *not* have happened. I am sure that if a man were hurt and starving in the desert and he called upon God to help him, God would not miraculously place a steak dinner before him. More likely he would direct some animal his way which could be caught and cooked, or even more likely direct some good Samaritan to help him who "luckily" went out of his way that morning.

Of one thing I was assured – God does not answer all our prayers according to our wishes. It would be horrible if he did. I certainly shudder to think of how some things would have turned out for me if he had answered some of my prayerful requests which I made when I was a young man. In the end one learns to trust to his greater wisdom. What happens as we grow into the knowledge of his love is that we make fewer demands and say with Christ; "Not my will but thy will be done." Our prayers become less and less a matter of self-interest and more and more a surrender into God's hands. That is the growth of faith.

Another of the fascinating corollaries of *activity* as constituting the material of the physical universe is that this activity contains within itself a dimension of the physical structure which we generally recognize as *time*. Activity is dynamic, which means, insofar as we can visualize it, that it is in motion or has motion as one of its inherent qualities. But motion as we know from the most elementary consideration of it always means changes of position during certain intervals and it is this concept of *during* or of duration which is the time element within activity. It is a difficult concept to understand, that is time as being one of the inherent qualities of the dynamic structures which constitute our material world. It is particularly difficult for those who are accustomed to think of time as some independent entity off by itself in which God exists and has existed as we have been taught "from eternity to eternity." But to realize now that time itself is a quality, (actually a dimension since like space it can be measured) means that God, unlike ourselves, does not abide within time or temporality, but that time is continuously created through the active expression of God's will which is also the activity principle of the material world. God thus creates time as he creates the material structures and in doing so he is also creating space since these structures have the space dimensions.

Now what did all this difficult and somewhat metaphysical discussion of time and space as being the dimensions of the physical world have to do with God and the faith in God? It removed certain blocks to understanding, and certainly to my own religious as well as to my scientific understanding it came as a most welcome revelation, in that a world of endless possibilities was opened up. There could be no limit, none whatsoever, to any growth and expansion of any new world of any universe which God might have in mind for man some day in the future. But much more important there was an immediate enlightenment concerning problems which, with others as well as with me, had been barriers to the growth of faith. One, for example, was the great number of human beings whom God was supposed to have under his love and care and the question as to how he could possibly keep so many in mind at once. The other was the problem of death itself and the question of how God could possibly return us into the time element after we had apparently stepped out of it in death.

To ask such questions is to raise the whole problem as to what constitutes existence. But I do not think we can ever answer that question. It is too basic for us to find terms and concepts in which it can be framed. All we can do with ultimate reality is to recognize its presence and then only if that ultimate reality expresses itself. Existence as we conceive it is always within the framework of time and space but now we must recognize that the God who creates time and space and puts it at our disposal must have his own existence upon a level which is not available to our understanding. We can say with certitude, "God is," but it is only because of his ability for self-expression that we can add that he has a personal reality.

There is a modern school of philosophy known as existentialism which, as near as I can discover, admits of there being a reality of sorts but refuses to see it as having any meaning. According to them it is just there, that's all, to be endured or perhaps enjoyed. The existentialists, poor things, have raised what is purported to be a philosophical question which they regard as very deep, and perhaps it is in a way since any context upon which it rests drifts away into a kind of infinity of negation. They say, "Why should there be something instead of nothing?" which is a question which raises the whole point of what constitutes existence. They want something explained in terms of something else within a familiar framework which in turn would be incapable of explanation. Actually what they are doing under high-flown philosophical pretense is what we are all in the habit of doing and that is projecting our own limitations upon God.

We, enclosed within a time framework, are unable to see how God is able to keep us all individually and personally under his care. To attempt to explain it would be to make the same mistake the existentialists make. But this I think we can say with assurance, and that is that since God is not under the same limitations of time, then time for him is something entirely different from what it is for us. Past, present and future are all spread out before him in a *now* which in our case is eternally fleeting. And the same must be true in the matter of space in which we find ourselves and also in the matter of numerity, the many many millions who compose the human race. Whether we understand it or not does not matter in the least – the important thing to see is that our limitations do not apply to God and that we need have no reservations as to his ability to love us individually and to restore us again in time at the resurrection.

I am inclined to believe that with the discovery of the material world as being dynamic in its nature instead of being composed of inert parts, scientific thought will come to take livingness more for granted in its physical system instead of taking, as it still does, lifelessness for granted. As I studied scientific thought and scientific method I quickly came to perceive that whenever the question concerning the origin of life is raised in a scientific discussion we are always asked to assume that we are dealing with a world which is initially dead. Somehow, somewhere, so goes the scientific explanation, fortuitous circumstances were such that life came about, generally in some primordial ooze or some other condition depending upon the particular theory suggested. I could never bring myself to accept that intellectually, much less to accept it religiously. The Christian who sees God as personal, and as having the personal dynamic at his disposal, does not need to inquire into origins, least of all the origin of life. God is a living God or he is nothing. The Christian believer takes life for granted, he recognizes it as a reality and takes joy in it. His problem is not that of life but of death. Death for him is a shocking, mysterious event and he stands appalled at its mystery. We speak of the blackness of death. What happens, we ask, when those whom we love suddenly depart? What happens to the soul, the animation, the ability to communicate? Above all, what happens to the love we have had for them and the love they have had for us.

We do not understand death because we do not understand life. How could we? If God is the God of life who gives us no terms in which to define it, then death can only be regarded as the negation of God. It is a state of non-being in which that very activity of God which created man in the first place has departed from him. Man then steps out of time and space which have been inherent in God's activity and he enters into the "outer darkness" of nothingness where he becomes a "lost soul" in the created scheme of things and from which God alone is able to rescue and restore him. I do not believe as I was once taught that he is sent to hell for his sins, or that he persists in some shadow world of half-life, the Sheol of the ancient Jews or the Hades of the ancient Greeks. I believe that in man's freedom to depart from God he can succeed so completely in his departure that he is able to alienate himself from the source of his creation and that therefore the creative activity which gave him birth and sustained him for a while is finally severed. Immortality is not a necessary adjunct of man's nature, though it could be if man maintained his connection with God. But "the wages of sin is death" which is not a punishment but a very logical consequence of the chaotic condition in which man must find himself if the very dynamic of his life which should always grow outward, falls back upon itself for lack of orientation. I cannot see how human life can possibly be sustained by God if man removes himself from God. It would be utterly horrible if man, in his preoccupation with self, continued to live forever. Only God's mercy permits man to eventually escape from himself in death.

This departure from life into the complete darkness of annihilation is said to have been the belief of the Apostle Paul. But it was also the great conviction of Paul, the "Fool in Christ", that through Christ death had been overcome. All it requires apparently is a re-orientation, "a repentance" as it is called in the Bible, for man to reverse his present course which is away from God. When he does so God's mercy which rises above all the natural laws of causality will once again enfold him and triumph over the evil into which he has fallen. Death, the last enemy will be overcome.

The God of the Old Testament

Though I always consider myself especially fortunate in that during the course of my life which has been beset with doubts and fears and even superstitions, I should finally have developed a philosophy which integrates the cross currents of my thinking, I do not mean that through my own mental efforts I have invented a structure of Truth but rather that it has been revealed to me according to my needs and at the stage of my spiritual development when I was ready to receive it. Truth, I was finally to discover, is something one enters into and is not merely knowledge as, for example, scientific truths written on the mind. But I am convinced that a deeper knowledge is always there waiting to be discovered and it comes to us in the same way that the solution of, say, a problem in mathematics comes to us. We bring to it our earnest effort and concentration, we look at it and bring to bear upon it our previous knowledge. Suddenly – flick! There is the answer. It was, as it were, out there waiting for us all the time, but to discover it we had to try most earnestly.

And so it is with the larger Truth which God reveals to us. It too is out there awaiting us, but, just as in a problem in mathematics, to solve it we must have had a preliminary knowledge. The lesser knowledge contributes its little share to the larger revelation. We may have to go through a somewhat simple and elementary knowledge of God before our present knowledge is widened. That is why, I suppose, that individual races and civilizations have to progress from partial stages, from a multiplicity of gods, to the One God, from there to a gradual and growing understanding of God's nature as finally revealed in Christianity.

Christianity could grow only out of Judaism. To all people of this world, both primitive and pagan, the knowledge of God is to some extent revealed. I know of no religion or religious cult in which there is not some measure of Truth. But into the Jewish civilization and Jewish culture a deeper knowledge of God found its way, and here again, this can only be regarded as God's revelation. They had every reason to think of themselves as "the chosen people."

The big theme which raised Judaism above other religions of their time was that of monotheism – The One God. But it was more than merely that. The idea of the one God was not altogether new – the Egyptians had adopted it for a while but it had fallen away. What was new in Judaism was more than the recognition of the One God, Jehovah. It was the conviction that this One God was actually *concerned* for them as a race. One can see here the persistence of the tribal God brought over from pagan beliefs. But historically it was a tremendous advance over paganism – the idea of investing this God with an actual concern, a personal regard, which is in fact an aspect of love – raised it to a religion to which one could respond without actual fear. It was a practical religion. Obedience was rewarded and disobedience was punished. Moreover it was racial. From each individual of the race an ethical conduct was demanded, and this ethical conduct was later codified into what came to be known as "The Law."

The Jews seem to have been a singularly gifted race. It may be that those first shepherd kings like their founder Abraham had felt a sense of isolation and even guilt, and under the desert stars had projected their souls toward the Infinite in search of Truth. Thus the revelation of the One God had come to Abraham as it does to anyone in search of Truth. It may have been a slow growth and it may have been a sudden surge of insight that came to Abraham as years later it was to come with greater revelation to the Apostle Paul. Abraham is said to have had "Faith" and that, with all its implications, is something new in religious history. It laid the foundation upon which, "in the fullness of time" the even greater concern of God for each individual member of the race could be revealed.

The civilizing and cultural effect of the new religion which had sprung up on the shores of the Mediterranean was to change the course of history. It produced a literature which, because it was God-centred, has never been excelled. It inspired courage, conviction, character, it gave us the thunderous prophets, the lyrical stories of Jewish women, the history of Kings and battles, the searching story of Job, the poetic psalms of David and the clever epigrams of Solomon. To my mind, the most beautiful of all, are those lovely legends of man's creation and fall with their poetic insight. But it was a literature nevertheless–God-centred, and God-inspired, but certainly not, as some still maintain, God-dictated.

Judaism, despite its insights and its expanding vision of Truth, was an immature religion. Even as a child must grow in wisdom and understanding into the higher concepts of God, so also must a civilization. From childhood to maturity is a steady growth, and if it were not so then we would have the suddenly flashing complete Truth thrust upon a people before they were ready to receive it. Religious understanding like culture must continually widen its horizons, but this, the Jews as a race, failed to do.

In *Tower in Siloam* I made much use of a quotation which I had read somewhere to the effect that "Man is unteachable at the point of pride." It is an obvious truth, but is also true that man is unteachable whenever he raises a barrier of any kind against being taught, whether this barrier is self-assertion, or arrogance, or smugness or pretentiousness – anything in fact in which the self is interposed between that which is given and that which should be received. And the Jews, lost in their preoccupation with that share of Truth which was their revelation and which had made them great and had given them their place in history, became no longer teachable. They raised a barrier against further knowledge of God and a deeper insight by their exclusiveness as a race. God had blessed them, and they were now superior to all the rest of the world. "We know. We were chosen. To us was given. We are custodians of the Truth," was their racial assertion. They might have added like a stubborn child, "No one is going to teach me anything or tell me what to do."

It was this racial self-assertion which stood in the way of spiritual development among the Jews. Individually there must have been many who had begun to feel the inadequacy of established Judaism, and it was certainly so at the time of the appearance of Christ. But on the whole, they allowed their faith to drift into formalism and their ethics into legalism. "The Law" had become paramount, something to be almost worshipped as a gift in itself from God. Certainly any violation of it was regarded as an offence against God. God in turn was regarded as the great cosmic legislator who was characterized above all by his justice. Obedience to the law thus brought its rewards and disobedience brought its punishments.

But how is man to love a God whom he fears? The Jewish religion as it has come down to us from the Old Testament was one based upon justice. Like all religions which fail to rise to the acceptance of the completely loving God, it tended to be anthropomorphic and visualized God in the image of man instead of seeing Man in the image of God. And out of the built-in justice which is the reliability and the consistency of the physical world, the Jews had derived a sense of justice which they attributed to God. From a consideration of the way things act, the cause-and-effect interpretation of physical process, they drew the concept of the just God, who had created it, the supreme law-giver who meted out punishment as well as reward. The devout Jew thus acted in accordance with God's law and received his reward and felt he had earned it. On the other hand if he acted in opposition to the law he received his punishment and felt in all justice it served him right. That was the God of Justice. But justice stands in the way of man's return to God.

As a child I was brought up to believe that the complete Bible was the word of God. I gathered from my early teachings that God had dictated every word to those who wrote the Scriptures even to the extent of correcting their spelling and that therefore not one jot or tittle was open to dispute. It is a belief which persists among many to this day. I still have relatives who take refuge from thought by responding with a quotation when asked for an opinion on spiritual matters. They will admit that although the idea of actual dictation may no longer be altogether tenable nevertheless the writers of the Bible were "inspired." Apparently this inspiration was direct from God and admitted of no personal bias or interpretation on the part of the writer. Human fallibility was thus ruled out in connection with the Bible and any approach to it had therefore to be one of unquestioning belief.

It took me a long time to outgrow this rigid attitude and my growth was attended with doubts and many misgivings. One does not lightly discard old beliefs. If the Bible, I would tell myself, is unreliable in some respects then the whole book is suspect. Where then is the anchor of faith? What is to be believed and what is to be discarded? It was not until I realized that God in giving man his freedom of self-possession had also given him the freedom to weigh evidence, to test and reject, that I began to see that a completely monolithic book from which there could be no departure would enslave man's spirit as well as his thoughts. He would be unable to grow in faith or in understanding. He could accept God but his growth of love would be inhibited by the compulsion to believe literally. It would all be cut and dried and we ourselves would become religious puppets, obedient and living according to rule but not permitted to adventure into faith.

I am being told from time to time by some of these earnest souls who still cling literally to The Book that much of it is "symbolical" and that those passages which make demands upon our credulity or those which violate our good opinion of God, must be interpreted "symbolically." To these I raise no real objection – if one holds, for example, that a symbolical Jonah was swallowed by a symbolical whale I am not the one to undermine their beliefs. But I point out that it means no more to me than a symbolical Jack climbing a symbolical beanstalk and that neither incident leaves me spiritually exalted. After all, one man's symbolism is another man's nonsense. Moreover the symbolical interpretation lends itself to any meaning which the symbolizer chooses. But when from some passage in the Old Testament God emerges as being stern and exacting, cruel and arbitrary, given to justice instead of love, then I say that such a presentation of God is false.

I do not undertake to assert in the face of those many sincere and earnest people who hold the complete Bible, Old Testament and New, to be the inspired word of God that it is untrue. Much of it must indeed have been inspired and those poetic myths concerning creation carry great poetic and spiritual Truth without becoming involved in the little factual truths with which science is concerned. But the concept of God presented to me by the Old Testament is no longer one which I can accept after accepting the one presented by Christ. My objection is that in the Old Testament, God is continually doing deeds resembling those of magicians. He turns staffs into serpents, he drowns mankind including innocent women and children in the great flood at the time of Noah, he commands the Israelites in their departure from Egypt, to invade Canaan and to put the cities, men, women *and children*, to the sword if they resist. He visits plagues upon the Egyptians, he makes trivial rules which the Isrealites are expected to obey and if they do not he punishes them. He is petulant, jealous, cruel, and tricky. Such is the image of God which for me emerges from the Old Testament. The anomaly between that early God of Judaic writings and the God of love and mercy as revealed by Jesus must surely be the cause of much distress to those who say that God is unchanging. It was certainly the cause of much distress to me. What I had to learn, of course, was that although God many not change, human concepts and understanding of him are changing all the time.

I realize that the Old Testament is a God-centred book, the story and literature of a God-centred people to whom God had revealed himself as the *One* God. But in the Jewish mind it was a concept which was still to a great extent undeveloped. The Jews were indeed a *chosen* people and their history and literature which has come down to us centres around this belief. It was the only religion of the ancient world from which Christianity could arise. It has deep insights and vision and we would all be poorer, indeed Christianity itself would be poorer, without the Old Testament as its background. Though it had developed into legalism and the Jews lived more by their code than by faith, yet among them from time to time arose those fervent prophets to whom God had revealed something of his own nature pointing toward a Saviour of mankind, a Messiah, and demanding of the Jews a greater understanding of God than that of a mere law-giver. "What doth the Lord require of thee but to do justly and to love mercy and to walk humbly with thy God?" declared the prophet Micah. But on the whole legalism had taken too great a hold. No doubt it kept them more or less disciplined but discipline alone will never prevent anyone from falling into perversions and we know from time to time the Jews would fall into the Baal worship of the Caananites from which they would be recalled by fervent prophets who predicted God's wrath and punishment upon them. I have no doubt that the idea of individual responsibility and individual salvation must also have been found among them but the conviction of their being the chosen people made their God into a tribal God and not one to whom they were personally related in terms of love. They did not seem to believe in any individual life after death, the reward for obedience to God's rules and regulations was material prosperity and a long life here on earth. The expected Messiah was to be a national liberator. The law by which they lived stood for the establishment. The accusation of blasphemy brought against Christ by the priesthood was because he was considered a political threat and a danger to all the accepted racial as well as religious concepts.

Most thoughtful Jews of today are quite willing to accept our Christ as another prophet, a humane and enlightened leader who was willing to die for his convictions. They are willing to see him as an ethical reformer who revealed God's nature even to the extent of his being a loving God as opposed to a merely just and legalistic God. But they refuse to see him as God personified, as "the Word made flesh". I was reminded of this just a short time ago in a conversation with an educated and enlightened young Jewish woman with whom I was discussing this very matter and I asked her why and if she was willing to concede all these great and loving qualities to Christ, the Jews would not accept him as more than just another of their prophets. The answer threw much light upon other discussions I had had with Jews at other times concerning this same question. Her answer, which was straightforward and honest concerning the acceptance of Christ, was simply, "But if we had, what would have become of us as Jews?"

Now that, I am inclined to believe, is consciously as in this case, or subconsciously in most other cases, the basis for the non-acceptance of Christianity on the part of the Jews at the time of Christ. They insisted upon their Judaism and they knew that the acceptance of Christ would destroy it. I have certainly known many Jews with a deep and devout faith in God and I think that in this modern age of progress among the Jews much of their faith has turned to a less legal and more personified God. Those I knew were certainly generous of mind and in conduct they were everything one could ask of Christians. But some ingrained Jewishness stood always in the way of their acceptance of Christ as Christians do. It was so deeply ingrained in their history that it led to the crucifixion of Christ himself.

Though I was not brought up as a Jew, I was very much brought up on the Jewish God, at least the God of the Old Testament, as my parents interpreted him. And my struggles, intellectual as well as spiritual, lay in the difficulty of abandoning those concepts which had become ingrained in childhood and later replacing them with the God of the New Testament as revealed by Christ. The difference between these two approaches to God which were great enough to lead to the crucifixion of Christ in the past should always, I think, be kept in mind in those discussions between fundamentalists and Christians in which the Loving Father of the Christian Gospel is quoted in the same breath with the Lord God Jehovah of the Old Testament tradition. The anomalies, the conflict between the two concepts is still so great that it gives rise to the cry, "In which God shall I believe?" The answer as far as I am concerned has become fixed in my convictions; *I will believe nothing which detracts from the love and goodness of God.*

That statement has become something of a formula in my life. It certainly simplifies the whole matter of belief or of doctrine or the interpretation of the Bible. If, for example, the Old Testament presents me with an image of God who is cruel and resentful and suspicious, I simply put it down to the fault of the Old Testament writer who, no doubt, meant well but could not see it any other way. I may have, as indeed we may all still have, at times doubts about God's goodness and love, as had the writers of the Bible, but I know that such doubts are due to the sin of withholding ourselves. Perhaps they are due to our inability in our present state of sin to accept God's love completely. Perhaps our image of him will always be clouded.

I believe that my rule of not believing anything which robs God of his love and goodness is a rule with which no one can find fault. It has certainly simplified my own thinking. It has given me a God as revealed in Christ who is not in the least concerned with justice. He is concerned only with love and mercy. For that matter he is not concerned with creeds and doctrine. Faith and trust rise above all theological systems since these, in the end are mere rationalizations of our personal approach.

Personality

Philosophical training dies hard. I found that in my religious growth I was obliged to devise a kind of rationale, a system of thought based on first principles before I could escape from some of the misgivings which had bothered me in my thinking. In the end it turned out to be a restatement of that wonderful passage from St. John's Gospel, "In the beginning was the Word."

I suppose that in any rational search for God we must start with the old philosophical concept – God is. It is a purely metaphysical concept since it is beyond the physical and is thus beyond our usual way of perceiving things in physical terms. As it stands it has little meaning since it does not enclose God in any attributes we can understand. We may say, God is, but we have not defined his *is-ness*, that is to say, the terms of his existence. But at least it is a starting point of thought, the assumption of an Ultimate Principle, a Prime Mover, a First Cause, always the aim of classical philosophy. It is only when we begin to clothe the concept of God to whom we have assigned existence with such attributes as power and purpose that he begins to be meaningful. Actually it is only when we say that he is personal, or that he has personality, that he becomes acceptable within our understanding.

To attribute only power to God does nothing more than include him in the collection of physical forces which science summarizes under a system of natural laws. When, however, we add that his power can be directed toward definite ends, that is to say, when we assign purposes or purposiveness to an all-powerful God, then he becomes personal and steps out of the sterile field of metaphysical thought into our human understanding. Insofar as we, who are also persons, learn to understand the purposes of God we will be able to understand our own selves and find our meaning since it must lie within the purpose of the Ultimate God who created us. We cannot escape this conclusion unless we deny the actual existence of a God of creation. If we do then we have no other choice but to regard ourselves as accidental products of natural laws and forces.

The recognition of the existence of a God of purpose, even an incomplete concept, is necessary as a context in our search for meaning. I have little patience with these self-nominated intellectuals who simply and shallowly assert that there is no God. They quite arbitrarily set limits to their thinking. I know from my own experience that God, above all the loving God, is very difficult to find, and I have a great sympathy and fellow feeling for those who search and fail because there is so much evil in this world that the face of God is often hidden. But those self-assertive knowers who make a cult of shallowness and proudly declaim their freedom from the superstition and bigotry which they generally associate with religion, are simply cutting themselves off from knowledge and are asserting ignorance as an intellectual virtue.

I am convinced that the Personal God is the ultimate reality underlying all things since I cannot make sense of any concept of reality which is not personal. Looking around me I see only persons as real. All else is fleeting and all else is subject to the basic law of change and destruction, (maximum entropy). But persons remain as realities though their physical means of expression undergo continual wastage and change. They grow up, they mature, they get old, they are subject to disease and even die. But we can love them as continuing realities throughout. At their deaths we are confronted with a mystery – they seem to have become removed from our experience and unless we want to believe that they are completely destroyed and that all love which we could give them and the love which they could give us is destroyed with their physical means of expression, we can still hope and believe that what was good in them is held in trust by the God of love and life of which they are a part.

I believe that Personality is a basic and ultimate concept because we have no terms in which we can define it. Personality is that which defines itself. It has its necessary means of expressing its purposes and although we can describe it we cannot find some further context of reality in which to give it meaning. Even in the matter of existence, when we say, "God is," the usual terms of existence, that is, time and space, are themselves created in that they are dimensions of the physical structure which God creates. But one thing is certain and that is that if personality did not have at its disposal some power to act, some means of communication and expression to which we could respond, we could never know whether it was there or not. The created world is the means whereby God reveals himself to us.

I have already discussed in *Tower in Siloam* the dynamic nature of the physical world. It was a discussion taken largely from other books by those scientists like Jeans and Eddington and Whitehead and Albert Einstein, and the reader is referred to them for further study and understanding. Certainly the concept of the material world being composed of some immaterial principle is by no means new in science. Nor, in religion, is the concept of God being the creator and author of our universe new. The power to act must certainly also be the power to create, and unless such power takes on meaningful forms, that is to say unless meaning is imparted to the forms and structures created, then there is no meaning ever available.

It is a most tempting subject to pursue. But it carries us again into metaphysical realms which are far removed from the real importance of the creative activity of God which is that any meaning abiding in his creations must arise out of the inner nature of God himself. I am convinced that this quality, this attribute, this inner nature, must be that of complete lovingness. It is only thus that we can accept him without becoming involved in objections, contradictions, and superstitions. The destructive power of any unlovingness, that is to say the destructive power of any evil which we can associate with God in any way whatsoever must violate our sense of his unity. It also violates our sense of consistency and rightness. It contradicts God's omnipotence as well as his perfection. It is certainly true of any of us that no matter how good and kind and loving we may be, a little evil blights and soils our perfection, and this little evil we will not concede to God. When I speak of the "destructive" power of evil I do not believe that evil has any power in its own right or that there is some principle of evil in this universe apart from God. I cannot believe in any department or spiritual realm presided over by some other being, some Satan or Devil who is opposed to God and his work. The old belief of my childhood that there was some area *into* which one of the Angels, Lucifer, could fall, and then in disguise tempt Adam, the first man, into oppositon to God, robs the omnipotent God of his omnipotence. The destructive power of evil to which I refer is simply the very dynamic of God himself which has been distorted and perverted by man who was given some of

God's creative power when he was first made in God's image.

I know very well that there are those who quote the scriptures to support their belief in a personal Devil and who point to the story of Christ's temptaton in the wilderness in which in the end he cried out, "Get thee behind me, Satan." But we can say this of ourselves when we know that we are being tempted by our own desires. As I see it, Christ, or possibly his biographers writing years later, were simply using the imagery of the day, for it was Christ who also said, "Out of the hearts of men proceed evil thoughts" and then after recounting some of the evil acts resulting from it he stated then "they came from within."

Now the existence of evil in this world is always the greatest problem of religious thought and the one which stands in the way of the acceptance of God. But if God is truly loving then the necessity of creating some being like himself who can love in return is already implied in that belief. For love is not ingrowing – it must extend outward toward some living creature who can not only become aware of love but can also love in response. And when God created man he must have extended to him some of that awareness which he had also extended into the whole created universe. But in the case of man he was given a self-awareness. Man had become aware of himself as a separate reality within his own possession to give or with-hold. This is a new freedom and is man's great distinction over every other living creation. It is a freedom which enables him to be truly loving.

It is tremendously fascinating to reflect upon the possibilities which had been opened up to this newly created creature into whom God had "breathed the breath of life" whereby he became a living soul. Life had already been given to other animals but to become a soul was to have life in its own right and to be released from the instincts and the too heavy effect of the environment to which other animals in the created kingdom were subject. Man had become a person as God was a person and thus he was created in the image of God.

Only persons are truly in God's image in the sense that they have the freedom to give or to with-hold. But to be a person also involves a sense of separation. It involves a separation from others as well as from God. This too, is part of man's freedom. He finds himself in a world in which he is something of a stranger and because he still has within himself much of God's image and God's love he is continually reaching out to overcome his sense of alienation. He is certainly not spiritually or intellectually satisfied with the condition in which he finds himself and most of his efforts in life are aimed at achieving a personal satisfaction in one form or another. In a universe in which he feels his alienation he tries to "fit in."

In Man's estrangement as we would expect, with the awareness of self and its freedom, the temptation to surrender to the gratification of self, would also arise. To yield to this is man's "fall" and his sin, but the freedom to sin is also the charter of his man-hood. The one thing God would not do in his love for man would be to reach in and destroy this freedom upon which the integrity of self rests. Nor, for that matter, would God change the physical system in which man had been placed, a system with reliable rules or "natural laws" without which man would not be able to exercise his freedom to act sanely and rationally.

There are further implications. One can see how this awareness of being a person separated from other persons and other creatures must have affected man's intellectual development along materialistic lines. The awareness of his own individuality and personal identity must certainly enhance his ability to separate one aspect of his environment from another and to see it in terms of cause and effect. He would be able to see consequences of his actions and bring a moral judgement upon them. He could think and rationalize in a new way and become aware of his relationships to others. It is no wonder that he was "given dominion over the fish of the sea, the fowl of the air, and all those creatures that creepeth upon the earth."

But at the same time he was destroying those things over which he had been given dominion. Even worse he was destroying himself. Man was becoming progressively evil in his preoccupation with self-love and self-service. The result was that all his purposiveness together with its dynamic expression became ingrowing. The self, and not God, had become the centre of reference and the distortions and perversions of man's creative power which had been given by God, were becoming more and more destructive. The built-in justice of the physical system with its cause and effect, its sin and consequences, would not fail to operate. Man's departure from God and his concern for the self had resulted in his own destruction. The wages of sin had become death.

It is all very tragic. Here is man, created "in the image of God" and at the same time "born in sin." He is a living paradox, a queer hybrid partaking of God's loving nature and yet living in the evil which he himself has brought about. Insofar as he loses sight of the personality of God he must regard himself as living within an impersonal system and being at the mercy of its mechanical laws. His sense of incongruity, of his paradoxical position within the scheme of things may sometimes give him a sense of humor when the departure from what he is and what he intuitively feels he should be is not of any great moment, but when the departure is great then he is also given over to the sense of tragedy. Doubts and uncertainties are then as much his lot as physical pain. The wages of sin is not only death, but ignorance.

Divine Justice

Only persons can sin. Although animals may have a fondness and affection for each other they are incapable of love in the sense that persons are capable of loving. They cannot consciously and deliberately give themselves for others. Sacrificial love is beyond them. And because they do not have the ability to give and with-hold as man has, they are incapable of sinning. We certainly never visit a moral judgement upon animals even though they may be perverse and disobedient.

I do not know why it should be that animals who are incapable of sin should nevertheless have to suffer some of its evil consequences. It may be that man, in his initial "fall" perverted not only himself but also the whole physical and organic environment. The gift of individuality, the separateness of being created a person is never so complete that it cuts us off entirely from our environment or from each other – after all, both man and his environment are part of God's creation. But a flaw in one part must affect another. It would certainly be an anomaly of creation if imperfect man had been set in a perfect environment. Paul, the Apostle, says something about the whole creation which "groaneth and travaileth in pain together." One thing however is certain in this life – the innocent continually suffer for the guilty. That alone denies the formal justice of God.

But then justice was never an attribute of God

in the first place. In my own development I had to rid myself of the idea of God's justice in the same way that I had to rid myself of the belief of a principle of evil apart from God. I can see now that wrath and retribution attributed to God was a product of the Jewish point of view as expressed in their Old Testament writings. The Christian church took over much of that point of view and much of it still lingers to stand in the way of our approach to God. There may be a moral justice within God's universe which rises above the usual reward and punishment of our actions within life, which is that since we are incapable of shedding our sins through our own efforts, divine justice demands mercy and forgiveness. But it cannot be just a casual overlooking of sin otherwise there would be no point in man's creation as a loving person in the first place. Divine justice calls for *sacrificial love* — man is to be remade in God's image so that he may reach his highest potential. And it is this sacrificial love which is revealed in Christ the Son of God. It was conscious giving and sharing, voluntary personal identification with others which is love at its highest. It involved suffering and sorrow and finally the surrender of life. The good-natured, grandfatherly type of God could not save man unless he were to be demoted to the status of a happy animal. It is the cross of Christ, with all that it implies which can bring man back into a living and life-giving relationship with his Creator. Man's sin is his denial of God and cannot be treated casually.

Let anyone ask himself what Christ would be to us, or for that matter, what would be left of him if he had not died on the cross. Could we possibly as weak, insignificant, and unimportant persons on this lonesome planet have ever found our own importance in God's eyes if we could not have risen through Christ's sacrifice into the fellowship with God? It is only through the explicit personality of Christ among us that we can relate again to the infinite Personality of God himself.

The divine justice which meets man's sin with love and mercy is by no means the same as that man-made justice, the law and punishment system derived from the material world although it may not be altogether illogical to attribute this type of justice to God since the world in which man lives with its causes and effects, which in human affairs is its rewards and punishments, was created by God in the first place. The Jews who had not risen to the understanding of a completely loving God, or perhaps it would be better to say had not as yet had the completely loving God revealed to them as he was to be revealed in Christ, would naturally see their God in terms of justice and as first and foremost a law giver. But unless this point of view is surmounted one cannot see the significance of Christ in human affairs. Justice stands in the way of our personal approach to him. His very divinity in those terms would keep us at our distance and prevent our personal fellowship.

The Old Testament justice certainly stood in the way of my approach to God. I had not read at the time those earnest and scholarly researches which had been written about Hebrew writings. Since then I have come to realize that they must be seen in their proper literary and historical perspective. Their inspiration and their godliness does not suffer thereby. The "Chosen People" were making their slow and stumbling way to the fulfillment of history where some day one of their race was to embody God himself. It would almost seem from reading their literature that they were being challenged by God and their response, sometimes good and sometimes bad, sometimes full of prophetic insight, God-centred it is true, but generally centred by a God seen in their own imperfect image, is undoubtedly a very precious literature. It was especially precious because in its preoccupation with God's relation to the human race it was preparing a spiritual environment in which Christ could come and could be received. "When the time was fulfilled" we are told, God sent his Son. But the time to be fulfilled was not calendar time; it was the preparation of the tilled soil in human hearts in which the old idea of a tribal God was to be replaced by the acceptance of personal God of love toward all men.

I know that this rejection of parts of the Scriptures on which we have been taught to depend will be met by some who will say of this book that it undermines faith. But it is to strengthen my own faith that I have made the rejections. It is not the superstitions and the folk tales of the Old Testament to which I object. I believe in miracles and especially in the miracles of Christ. It is unthinkable that if we accept Jesus as the Son of God that he could not do the miracles attributed to him, for certainly without having the power of God at his call and disposal at all times he can never be regarded as having made any sacrifice for us but was merely a victim of circumstance. But there is a big difference between the miracles of Christ and those attributed to Moses, when for example, he turned his staff into a serpent. My objection to that kind of miracle is not that God could not do it but that it is not in his nature to do tricky things like that. Christ could cleanse the leper and restore sight to the blind because they were miracles of compassion which revealed the forgiving power of God. They were not meant to impress sinners with fear and awe of some unseen power. To astound us into a belief in God was one of the last things that Jesus wanted to do, in fact he asked some of those whom he cured not to mention it because there was always a tendency to regard him as a healer only. I may believe in the Old Testament story of the flood, since there certainly seems to be geological evidence that there once was a great flood in Asia

Minor, but I certainly don't believe that God designed it to punish the inhabitants of the earth whom he regretted ever having created. A god like that is just too heartless to believe.

I very well recall as a boy how the earthquake which hit San Francisco in 1906 was regarded by the more pious ones as a punishment from God upon a particularly sinful city and I also remember wondering at the time just why he should have picked San Francisco. I was told that other cities were in line for later calamities unless they mended their ways. And I have no doubt that when the cities of Sodom and Gomorrah were lowered into the Dead Sea by a similar earthquake, their destruction was also attributed to the punishment of God in Biblical times as was San Francisco in my time. But again I certainly do not believe that God acts that way. It violates my faith in the integrity of God's love. It is certainly better to believe in the integrity of God than in the integrity of the Scripture.

When I came to the New Testament where we are given a different image of God than in the Old, I was no longer faced with the same doubts and unbeliefs. The events of the life of Christ and the story of his miracles were in complete conformity with the new concept of the merciful God whom he was revealing. Jesus as the embodiment of God brought into the reality of human experience not only God's love and mercy but also his saving power to overcome the sin into which man had fallen. The New Testament regarded as a human document written years after the life of Christ and by different disciples at different times, depending as it does upon tradition and perhaps faulty memory, may have its little anomalies and contradictions, but they are not contraditions concerning the central figure of Christ himself. I have no doubt that we have an accurate account of what he said and did and it is consistent in every respect.

There is only one instance to my mind which is inconsistent with the character of Jesus and this I attribute to human fallibility on the part of the Gospel writer.

I refer here to that passage – or is it a parable – in the Book of Matthew concerning the last judgement, in which after the sheep have been separated from the goats the Son of Man consigns those who have not received him in this life into "the everlasting fire prepared for the devil and all his angels." I do not understand how this passage found its way into the one, the only one, of the four Gospels. In my own life and faith I find that it must be reinterpreted or I must dismiss it as completely alien to everything Jesus taught and stood for. The Christ who is our hope and comforter and who told his followers in parting; "Lo, I am with you even to the end of the world" is not going to change into a fiery avenger at the end of the world. We are told by scholars of the Bible that the passage has been lifted almost bodily from the Book of Enoch, one of the apocryphal books which was too apocryphal to be included in our present Bible. I am inclined to think that after the half century or so since the death of Christ when this Gospel of Matthew was written some of our present attitudes of vengeance and punishment were already finding their way into the Christian tradition. We are told that the apocryphal books were never designed to extend knowledge but to nourish piety, and although I may appreciate their imagery and the majesty of their language, I must say that I have found precious little piety in them for myself. And certainly this passage with its promise of eternal punishment denies the loving character of God as well as of Jesus. Eternal death, the removal of the gift of life, the "outer darkness" of annihilation – those are things I can believe in as the logical consequence of man's defection from the purpose of his Creator. But if I am going to follow my resolution to believe only in God's love and goodness, then I will not believe in any sadistic eternity of punishment. The Christ who said at the time of his crucifixion "Father forgive them for they know not what they do" cannot, even in our own perverted concepts of justice and retribution, condemn humans for crimes they did not know they were committing. He knew that they were blind and that the wages of sin are not only death but also blindness and insensitivity and lack of compassion, all of which are punishment enough in that they deny the goodness of life and with it life itself.

Salvation

"Though I have the gift of prophecy and understand all mysteries and all knowledge . . . and have not love, I am nothing."

I sometimes think of that passage on those occasions when I tend to sit back in private satisfaction and say, "Well, I have finally acquired a coherent and rational outlook on life, one which is intellectually satisfying and philosophically adequate." It is an attitude which has finally escaped the fears which were instilled into me in my childhood and the threats of those early days, the revivalists, who called the sinners to repentance with the ominous "Tomorrow it may be too late." It gives meaning to my life because it gives purpose to God. Philosophically it answers the question of the existentialists as to *why* there should be something instead of nothing; morally it answers the question as to why there should be such a thing as evil because it attributes to God a complete lovingness.

But a philosophical or intellectual outlook in itself is always incomplete. What it lacks is that God's love should be brought into the reality of human experience. It is all very well to speak of the God of love and to think of sin as something resembling a metaphysical condition. But in our daily lives we need the consolation of *personal love.* We need the comfort of his intimacy, the sense of his nearness. We need to feel that he also knows about the painful and sorrowing consequences of sin. And I was to find that it is here, and here only, that the appearance of Christ as the Son of God, puts the seal of completeness upon our thinking and meets our needs. Christ had become the cornerstone of my structure, intellectual, spiritual, and personal.

The more I learn about other religions the more I realize that Christianity is the only realistic religion. It is the only one which faces up to the problem of evil. Unlike other moods and cults it does not evade evil, or attempt to explain it away or accept it as a law of nature to which we must be sorrowfully resigned. Christianity looks evil in the face and unreservedly states that it is with us and that it has no business here. It promises that in the mercy of God, evil will be overcome. The ultimate evil it states is death, and this too will be overcome and man will be restored to his life within the living God.

I can now understand why it should be that death, the wages of sin, is a logical consequence of man's defection from the God of life. Insofar as he drifts away from the source of life he must also drift into the non-life which is death. All his physical pains, his diseases, his doubts, his distresses, his fears and anxieties, his sorrows in parting from those he loves, are, as it were, symptoms of his spiritual malady leading to his final separation from God. I do not think that any of us in our present condition can ever have a complete understanding of the significance of Christ. We cannot, in our dulled perceptions, read the mind of God, but we can at least understand something of his love and purpose. But to understand this there is one central belief, one might almost say, one central point of doctrine, even dogma, which we must accept, and that is that Jesus Christ, who like ourselves was a person, was also the Son of God.

I know that for many in this materialistic age this is a difficult belief. That God, a somewhat nebulous cosmic principle should actually appear in physical form as a human being is just too much like one of the fairy stories of our childhood where animals became princes and pumpkins became carriages. But even more, in our day and age, it is, as the trade magazine of the United Church in Canada recently explained in refuting the story of the Virgin Birth, "unscientific." But that is just the very thing that makes Christ acceptable as the Son of God. Science, after all, is the study of the usual, the phenomena which we can account for by applying the regularities always observed, that is to say, the natural laws. But we overlook the fact that the natural laws are of God's making, and he can supercede them at any time with an unusual event. The event can be so unusual, in fact, as to be unique and therefore beyond scientific classification. Christ was indeed unique. There is only one Christ and the great glory and wonderment of his appearance is that he was not scientific. We could certainly never understand Christ or accept him as a personal saviour if we could explain him scientifically. He came from beyond our usual scientific system, and he *entered* the human race by breaking into the historical continuity of generation at the time of his birth. It was an act of creation on the part of God in which the causal sequence we are familiar with was interrupted and a new man appeared on the historical scene.

The incarnation of God in Christ has been regarded by many as a great mystery. But is it after all a greater mystery than our own presence here which we take for granted? The ability of persons and above all the ability of the Personal God to act, to communicate, makes its appearance as matter and as the material world. That the Word should become Flesh is manifested in us as it was in Christ. The amazing thing about the Son of God dwelling among us is not so much that he became a person like ourselves but that he was, in our experience, an entirely new kind of person. He was without sin. He was a person, who like ourselves had the self within his own possession but he did not yield to the insidious temptations of self. Not even in his concern for his fellowmen did he surrender to what might have pleased them such as the material benefits implied in the temptation to turn stones into bread. He did not use his powers to do those magic-like tricks which Moses had used before Pharaoh to impress his fellowmen with God's power and he did not entertain any scheme of grandeur and empire which would certainly have been regarded by the Jews as a fulfilment of their dream and promise.

Though Jesus overcame temptations they were very human temptations nevertheless and the fact that he was obliged to face them places him in our midst as a person like ourselves. The New Testament continually emphasizes the fact that he was "tempted as we are," and this above all relates him to us in human-ness. The most appalling thought that can enter our minds is that of Jesus failing. We ourselves have been created in God's image and have failed and fallen but there is hope for us. But if the Son of God had failed there would be no hope for man. Mankind, an incident in history, would have gone down to utter destruction.

Our knowledge of the humanity of Christ, his temptations and his suffering the consequences of sin with us, brings him very close. But it is through his divinity that we are able to penetrate the veil which separates us from God. For if we over-emphasize the humanity of Jesus he becomes just another man, a high-minded prophet who sacrificed himself for his ethical principles and whose example we should follow. If, on the other hand we over-emphasize his divinity he becomes as distant as God himself is distant. It is because he too lived within a kind of paradox as The Son of Man and as the Son of God that we can give him our compassion and know that he can give us his. Knowing that he was The Son of God, we can give him our complete trust.

The difference between Jesus and ourselves was that although he had the freedom to sin, he did not sin. He was finally the perfect man, the prototype of the man which God must have had in mind in those distant days when he first created the mythical Adam in the mythical Eden. For Jesus was a man who embodied God's complete lovingness. His concern was never for himself or for some tribe self-excluded from the rest of God's children. His only wish was that his fellowmen who had turned away from God might re-establish the bond of kinship with their God so that they might be enabled to say as he said of himself, "I and the Father are One."

There is no doubt that Christ was perfectly aware of his unique significance in human history. He has no hesitation of speaking of himself as the Son of God and apparently the belief and confidence in his Sonship was all he asked of his disciples or of those whom he healed and whose sight he restored. There is never in all his teachings a single suggestion that he himself stood in need of God's mercy and forgiveness. He had no hesitation in forgiving others their sins though this would naturally infuriate the Jews. That one of themselves, Jesus, the carpenter's son should arrogate to himself the right to forgive sins was utter blasphemy in their eyes; but they were faced with the astonishing fact that when he did forgive people their sins then the consequences of those sins were also wiped out and their diseases fell away.

On the other hand, Jesus as a person and having as all persons must have an awareness of personal integrity and with it the awareness of the separation from others, was obliged to continually project himself in spirit to God so that the bond between himself and the Father might not be weakened. Else why should he pray?

One feels a great compassion for Jesus, a fellow feeling, in the thought that he too had to pray to God. One of the consequences of sin is that sense of alienation, even of guilt, which arises from continual self-preoccupation. Though Jesus did not sin, nevertheless when he launched himself into a world in which sin abounds, he became a person and accepted all the evils resulting from man's sin without partaking of it. This is his sacrifice in our behalf.

One can understand why Jesus, although aware of himself as the Son of God, would nevertheless have to pray to his Father in Heaven. In his younger days he could not have known the suspicion and spite and final suffering which he was to know later. But he lived in a sinful world and he must have found it all very disheartening. We know, for example, how very disheartening even the morning news can be – one long recital of hatred and cruelty and violence and disaster, and it would almost seem as if God had turned his face away from humanity and left men to their fate. And I have no doubt that Jesus was often in the greater consciousness of man's defection from God, heavy-hearted and discouraged. In his book, *The Meaning of Paul for Today*, C.H. Dodd speaks of these prayers of Jesus: "The lonely prayers on Galilean hills by night, the exultation of the Spirit when He cried, 'I thank Thee Father, Lord of Heaven and Earth,' and the agonizing supplications of Gethsemane, 'Abba, Father, Thy will be done.' " They are infinitely touching when we consider them as coming from the Son of God who loved us enough to join in our distress.

Doubt, discouragement, boredom, fear, sorrow,

the departure of meaning, the lostness of the spirit, even the final agony of despair – such are the consequences of sin which humans undergo. The wages of sin are by no means only physical ones. They are also spiritual and I ask myself which of these Jesus was also to know before he submitted to that final suffering and indignity of the cross. It seems almost blasphemous to suggest that Jesus, who was one with God, also faced the uncertainty of doubt and the struggle for meaning. But we know nothing of his early days. We know nothing of his development and of that growing faith of which he seems to speak at first hand when he tells us that it grows from a small seed into a large tree. He could not have known as a little boy that he was the Son of God and that he was destined to be the saviour of mankind. Personally I take comfort from the thought that he also had his spiritual struggles, and my heart can go out to him because in fellow-feeling I know his heart can go out to me.

It would almost seem as if there was some kind of cosmic drama being played out when God sent his Son into the human scene for our salvation. It is evident that when Christ, the Son, identified himself with us that he was to experience our human suffering. But where does *our* salvation enter into this for it is also evident that the mere historic act of Christ's sacrifice need not affect us. Somehow or other, we too were to become involved and we would have to become involved in such a way that our integrity as free persons would not be destroyed. Compulsion could not be introduced into the problem of our salvation in any way whatsoever. Fear and punishment were the very things from which we were to be saved. Life was not to be threatened but to be given more abundantly.

Only in the recognition of God's Son voluntarily entering into his identification with us can we begin to understand the plan of salvation. It elicits from us a personal response. It is not a demand. Christ's "Behold I stand at the door and knock," is the great tribute he pays to manhood. It calls to us to identify ourselves with him as he with us and this can only be done by an act of faith. Mutual identification of Christ in man and man in Christ must then in all logic restore us from the bondage of sin.

This mutuality in which one person enters the spirit of another is of all things the most important since it strikes deep into the nature of love itself. If there is to be any salvation of man at all then the sacrifice of Christ for our sake is the only possible event which could ever take place to bring it about. When man identifies himself with sinless Christ he returns to the trust in God which he had originally lost when he ate of the Tree of Knowledge. It must follow that if Christ arose from the dead, then the man who identifies with Christ will also arise from the dead. He does not fall within sin's evil consequences. He may still be within a world governed by sin and in this life his death is still inevitable. But if Christ is what he declared himself to be : "I am the resurrection and the life. He who believeth in me shall not perish," then man, through Christ will not perish.

When I was a boy I was taught the doctrine of atonement. Christ, we were told, was above all innocent. As such he could take upon himself our sins and accept God's just punishment for our sake. Evidently God demanded, apparently so as not to lose face, that somewhere, somehow, somebody had to suffer, and Christ had acted as a whipping boy so that we could now be free of God's wrath. It is a most horrible doctrine and whatever it may have done to us as children in the matter of our approach to Christ, it certainly did not enhance our good opinion of God. Such pagan beliefs die hard because we are all still more or less obsessed with a sense of justice as an ultimate quality in the universe. In the end however one rises above such teachings but I still have to think of the doubts and confusions raised in my young impressionable mind by such teachings.

Faith, trust, confidence, loyalty – these are all aspects of our personal identification with our fellow-men. One sees these in one degree and another in our daily life for they are all in the end different aspects of the love which holds us together. I ask myself, for example, why a man places his arm affectionately over the shoulder of another. Is it not to indicate friendship, a gesture of *identification* which tells better than words that there is a sharing of feeling? And all sympathy and all compassion is similarly that fellow-feeling in which one person actually enters the personality of another. To give trust and confidence is to have faith; it is to yield the self into the other's hands.

In my religious thinking I no longer fight for that intellectually satisfying rationale whereby I once sought to love the Lord, my God, with all my *mind* as well as with my heart and soul. As far as I am concerned, the problem has been settled – my concern now is to strengthen faith, to stabilize a foundation of trust which never falters. Alas it is not always so easy. Convictions tend to fade and resolution grows dim. It is all very well to say that having once acquired faith in Christ and having received insights into God's grace one is now invulnerable. But, in the busy course of life such assurance tends to become eroded. It may be that this assurance is too much self-assurance, a lingering sin which blurs the very glass through which, as St. Paul says, "we see darkly." It may well be that it is only when we are thoroughly beaten by our own efforts, when in the fell clutch of circumstance we face hopelessness and defeat, that we are really aware of God's grace. It is certainly true that when we are most helpless we stand most in need of love and can become most aware of it.

I have met people at one time or another in my life, simple, unaffected ones who had certainly not had my advantages in experience and education, and I have stood in envy at their quiet acceptance of God's love and their unquestioning trust in the ultimate goodness of his ways regardless of sorrows and illness which they had to endure. They seemed to have a talent for trust which did not waver in the winds of life. In my own life there have been times when I also have known that peace "which exceedeth all understanding," – when the sense of God's nearness was very real. Those are the days to live for. But I don't suppose that in this world which abounds in sin, we are permitted to live for long in any quiet haven of peace or to be lifted up for long in spiritual exaltation. The world is too much with us. Fatigue, the declining vigour of years, an attack of indigestion, a poor night's sleep, the morning news – such things becloud our vision and it is consoling then, to know that even though Jesus may not have undergone them in the same way, at least he knows all about them. Life is a struggle for faith. I often take consolation in the thought of Peter, the bungling disciple of Jesus who every now and then fell from faith, even to the extent of denying his Lord on the night before the crucifixion. Yet he was the one who first said, "Thou art the Christ, the Son of the Living God." The human weakness of those first friends of Jesus brings the difficulty of our own present acceptance into perspective. If in addition we feel that even Jesus in his years of development and growing realization of his destiny and his place in God's plan also had his struggles, then we can feel comforted.

What we sometimes regard as the loss of faith may actually be a struggle for a higher level of faith. Apparently we are not permitted to sit still. Growth and development seem to be the law of personality. I often think of that splendid passage in W. Russel Maltby's book where he says, "God's wind and weather are always at work to seek out the perishable elements in our structure, and time and again, when we longed only for finality and repose, we are required to rise and rebuild, or strengthen, or repair." So it seems to be with our faith. There are times when it seems to disappear altogether. But I have found that it is there nevertheless. Like the love we cherish for someone very dear which seems so casual and even indifferent in the day to day hum-drum of life, it rises in a tremendous surge when the one we love is in trouble.

Conclusion

In concluding this book I ask myself just why I should have written it and what it all adds up to. I have certainly said nothing new. It has been in a way a description of an adventure in search of Truth and I have mentioned some of the difficulties and pitfalls I have encountered in making my way through a sceptical and scientific and very materialistic age. My interest in writing this account is what I have already said, that of sharing experience with others so that they may not find themselves too much alone if they happen to be travelling the same way. I find somewhat to my surprise that in my journey through religious thought I have actually returned to the fundamentalism of my childhood in the matter of Christ and Christian doctrine. Those early shibboleths of my Sunday School days concerning salvation and repentance, and about the Jesus who was the Son of God and who died for our sins have all become acceptable. But in a new way. They have become acceptable only within the ever-growing insight of God's love. Love was the fundamental element which had been left out of my fundamentalism.

Each of us has his own approach to the God of Truth and each of us sees in Christ some reflection of ourselves because he reflects all men. And if in this book I appear to have undermined some of the faith of others by casting doubt upon the validity of certain parts of the Scriptures it is only so that those other parts which reveal the lovingness of God might not be obscured. For, if after all, the collected books and letters which we call our Bible is a collection of human documents which are a growing revealment of God, then that to me is its goodness and its glory. I quote again from Russell Maltby's "The Significance of Jesus," where he says; "Revelation is not less truly God given because it is not dictated but discovered. . . . We can follow the conflict of true and false as they strove together in the minds of good men." For myself I feel that we cannot have spiritual freedom if we regard the Scriptures as dictated and although I tend most of all to discount the literal truth of The Old Testament, I am aware that the New Testament in which the Truth concerning God is finally revealed, is itself a series of human documents.

The amazing thing about the four Gospels themselves is their consistency in dealing with Christ. When one considers the lapse of years between their actual writing and the death of Jesus those little errors in the timing and telling of events which have crept in are surprisingly minimal. But there are no contradictions in the delineation of the character of Christ himself. Whatever literary faults we may encounter in the Gospels the writers did not impute any character to their central figure of Christ which was not there in actuality. I remember arguing this matter years ago with some students who maintained that because of little factual disagreements in the Gospels that the whole thing was contrived. Christ then was not the saviour of mankind but merely another character in literature albeit great. They argued that whoever his prototype may have been he had been idealized and romanticized by his biographers into a person who was never real.

But those young men did not know much about life and greatness and probably not even much about literature. The heroic characters of great writers like

Shakespeare and Goethe and Homer, the Hamlets and the Fausts and the Ulysses' shrink into little human insignificance beside the man, Christ. The possibility that four men, relatively un-lettered themselves and writing years apart could have invented a man such as Jesus cannot be entertained by scholarship. The one thing I believe with all my mind as well as with all my heart is that Jesus actually existed in the human history and that he was what he claimed to be, the Son of God who was sent for our salvation which is the escape from evil.

In the very nature of life there must always be many things we can never know. We cannot rationalize faith and among us there will always be differences of opinion. But the great joy of Christianity is that it is great enough and wide enough to permit its followers to unite in faith even though they may differ in opinion. We may have convictions but we need not on that account have dogma. Doubts and differences may still arise but with faith there is always that companion, hope.

Though I may have been poorly taught in my childhood it was well meant. "The fear of God is the beginning of wisdom" was something which it was the parents' duty to impart. Perhaps indeed it was the beginning of wisdom. I often wonder to what extent we would search for Truth and for the meaning of life, and for God's love if we were not driven to it by self-concern. It may be that in our very sin of self-concern we are led to the abandonment of self. It may be that in our futility we find salvation. "They that are whole have no need of the physician."

That is why I speak only for myself. Out of the past, out of my childhood came good things also – memories of love and sharing, of sympathy and kindness, of school and Sunday school, of creeks and flowers and fields of grain, the charm of the prairies

– I could write a long book about those lovely days. For they too are the material of which we build our lives, they too point to larger insights and understanding. We seem in a way to live in a kind of cycle of life – we return in the end to the simple unquestioning beliefs of childhood. But they have been winnowed and refined during the adventure. And because of the dynamic nature of life and the law that we must always grow and expand we never quite reach that "finality and repose," and therefore, I suppose, we will always be reaching out, questioning, inquiring, and sometimes doubting. Yet there is always that key of which Bunyan speaks, called Promise, which unlocks the Castle of Doubt.

Promise is valid only if there is an underlying trust. Doubts and discouragements notwithstanding, the hope which is implied in promise has never disappeared in my own life. Some day I hope the veil of ignorance will be swept away and we shall see "face to face." But for the present I am not at all sure that I want to be completely quit of doubts and difficulties. I do not like the thought of using God for my own comfort something like a tranquilizer pill. When things no longer trouble me I get worried that I may be basking in spiritual laziness. On the other hand they can become too troubled and one calls on God for help. I have found then that there is often a sudden burst of enlightenment which gives happiness for days. It is in that kind of experience, the dark as well as the light, which makes me feel that God is working within us.

Fear is a concern for the self, and so, on a higher level is that urge within us to seek Truth and personal salvation. I know that throughout my life I have resented fear and have reacted against it, and although I do not think there are any of us in this life who can rise to that love of which the disciple John speaks when he says, "perfect love casteth our fear" we can certainly reach moments from time to time when we feel the nearness of God and fear vanishes entirely. Even within those drab intervals when the petty aches and discomforts of declining years insidiously creep in with their plaguey self-concern which is a type of fear, there is still the comfort of knowing that underneath are the everlasting arms, and that nothing, but nothing, can ever really happen to us.

If someone were to ask me today just where I have reached and what in the end is the result of this journey in search of Truth, I could not give any very expicit answer. In the attempt to identify with Christ one naturally enters into a code of conduct which is based on the faith and fellowship with him. It certainly rises above all the rules and commandments whose violations were once held before me as a list of sins. One feels free of sin though recognizing that we are still subject to it and that we live in a world in which sin abounds. But the sense of fellowship confers a feeling of security and worth.

If I were to give advice to someone who wanted to be given an outline of Christian conduct I would say, Be yourself. Go ahead and lead your regular life whether you are butcher, baker, or candlestick maker, or for that matter, banker or broker, but never do anything which will undermine the faith of others. It is what we live by in our relationship with each other and it is our salvation in Christ. It is the most precious gift within the integrity of man for through it we have the freedom to give ourselves in trust to God and to each other. In your conduct then you will not cheat your neighbor in a business deal or betray or desert a woman who loves you. Such things destroy faith and if you destroy it in others you will not be able to have it within yourself.

To have freedom is to have the more abundant

life, and we are told again and again that the truth shall make us free. It is a freedom to develop according to our talents and even according to our eccentricities, because we are freed then of the neurotic concern for the self to which we have attached so much importance. We begin to realize then our much greater importance within God's love and our reality within ultimate dimensions.

Those ultimate dimensions used to bother me greatly. I have come to realize however through my knowledge of science and my reflections upon the nature of the substance which underlies the material world, that we as persons are not really limited to the usual dimensions and that someday, like God, may have our existence in other terms than time and space in which we are at present confined. That is why we can experience what we call the *nearness* of God. That is why we can say of him that he is omnipresent and can love each of us individually;

> "When we speak of God as omnipresent we usually come away with the notion that God can be in more than one place at the same time. Omnipresence is not a spatial term – it is a personal one. It means that God is near every one of us and the only thing that can separate us from him is our own self-will".

That is a quotation culled from a local newspaper and I think it is beautifully profound. We tend to visit our own limitations upon God and because of that we cannot see how it can be possible for God to hold each of us in his concern among the many, many millions of people who inhabit this earth. But then how is it possible that among the many, many million, of people here on earth each of us can hold himself within his *own* concern? It is really quite remarkable when we come to think of it. And yet it is only because of that ability whereby personality reaches out to personality, whether it is to each other or to God, that love becomes possible since then the concerns become mutual.

Some of us have one conception of sin and some of us another. In my motley collection of friends and others whom I happen to know sin seems to vary with their spiritual development. One I know holds that the greatest offence against his maker is to go fishing on Sunday and for another it is to have a blood transfusion. Others again swear by the Ten Commandments and not much else. Some of the revivalists have a list of prohibitions, and insist upon our believing the most outrageous things or face the penalty of eternal wrath. One can approach them with tolerance and charity but also say, "How can you possibly think so meanly of your God? Surely, on your own terms, the One who created us and loved us enough to give himself in sacrifical love through his only Son so that because of our perversity we might not be lost in the pit of annihilation, cannot be concerned with such trivial little acts. Heaven knows there is already enough punishment in the physical and social environment with its cause and effect consequences and it is just from these we are to be rescued. How can you possibly approach in love and trust, a God whom you fear and regard with apprehension? Surely Christ on the Cross freed us from such pettyness. Go and catch yourself a big trout for Sunday dinner and if you get into an accident on the way home, let me give you some of my blood for your present life, as Christ gave his for our eternal life."

Christianity is the coming religion. I cannot see any other which can possibly take its place. Our history has been one long development toward it from primitive witchcraft, driving out the devils of woods and jungle, through mythology, cults, and philosophies, the worship of strange deities – some horrible demanding the sacrifice of infants, others benevolent promising a paradise or happy hunting grounds, gods of war, gods of fertility, gods of justice – we seem to have discovered them all. We are God-searching creatures in this material world of wind and waves and trees and animals, and our restless search will not be ended until we find the God of love. There is nothing higher and any attempt to find another religion will fail because it is not in accord with the demands of our own basic natures.

I do not know how the new Christianity will be brought about. Some may say that we have already had Christianity for two thousand years and there is nothing new about it. That is true of many individuals who from the very first have found their joy and their realization within it. But is it not also true that Christianity has been formalized and institutionalized so that the personal worship of God which Christ himself predicted as coming, "Neither in this mountain nor in Jerusalem . . . but *in spirit and in truth*" has become unavailable to many who are searching? Institutions and efficiency, like bureaucracy, are always the foes of personality. And rightly or wrongly there is a tendency today, especially among young people, to associate the church with its forbidding aspects of the past.

What is being sought today is a religion without fear or compulsions and a feeling of togetherness, and this is just what Christianity can give. It was always inherent in the church but the church somehow seems to have frightened young people away. They have not yet discovered Christianity in its higher Truth and there is a spiritual vaccum into which have moved the weirdest cults in which fervour replaces depth and perversions thrive. Lacking Christianity's courage which realistically faces up to evil, they have devised escapist tricks like transcendental meditation and mushroom drugs. But such things pass and sooner or later Christ must come into his own.

One thing is certain; evil is always self-destructive and if we as a civilization are going to continue to drift into cults and superstitions and perversions, and for that matter, into the worship of the non-God, Materialism, we will bear witness to that worship in our collective acts. The ominous predictions concerning the self-destruction of mankind are by no means fantasy. As we well know there are today ever more frequent warnings from educated and thoughtful men that some kind of Armageddon threatens our civilization if socially and spiritually we continue as we are going.

I have never been able to follow those earnest students of the Book of Daniel and the Revelations who seem to be able to pinpoint the time and place of the great battle and predict the outcome. Apparently according to them the Devil and all his legions will not stand a chance although they will put up a pretty good fight while it lasts. After that Christ will reign. But I cannot see much difference between their victorious kingdom of God and that visualized by some of the more idealistic communists. Comes the revolution or comes the resurrection, the end result seems to be the same – a materialist Utopia. Presumably there will be enough good things there for everybody then and all will lead a happy life. Righteousness will be *enforced*. Inequities and injustice will simply not be permitted.

But I ask myself just where in such visualizations is that wonderful creation in the image of God, man himself? To this creature, in the very charter of his creation, was given the ability to love which is also the freedom to sin. Is this freedom to be taken from him? In that case he is destroyed as man. His destiny then is to crawl upon the face of the earth like a happy insect, eating and sleeping and perhaps with his superior mind devising and building for his further satisfactions. Indeed there are already some who on contemplating the distant galaxies and the infinite possibilities of outer space hold that man is nothing else than an intelligent insect.

I do not believe of God that he will turn the stones into bread. It is my belief and hope, as it is that of all Christians, that sin will some day be overcome with all its attendant evils. But it will be done with God's help and not by force or heavenly fiat. Our salvation, I am sure, lies not in some pearly-gated utopia in this life or the next, but in entering into the security of God's love, of becoming one with him while still maintaining our individual identities. It will be a triumph of the spirit – the rest will look after itself.

Just what this rest may be I have not the faintest idea and I sometimes think that Christ did not know either. He was a person like ourselves and persons are subject to limitations of knowledge. He knew of course that future life there would be on a different level from this, there would be, for example, neither marriage nor giving in marriage, but beyond that and saying that in his Father's house there were many mansions, he told us nothing about it. It is probably just as well. We collect so much junk in the course of our lives, some of it so precious that it is almost a relief to re-echo the old cliche; "Well, you can't take it with you." Possessions are always associated with anxiety – we protect them from theft and breakage and fire with such concern that we are finally happy to abandon them to those treasures upon earth "where moth and dust doth corrupt."

The real treasures we hope to take with us are the free ones – those beyond any private satisfaction or pride of possession. They are the shadings and nuances of the beauty we already find in the world in which we live. They are the sweep and wonder of its outer space, the charm of children, the loveliness of women and the rugged dignity of men. Above all they are those whom we have loved, complete in their own individualities which made each so fascinatingly different from the other.

Such is our faith and our hope – held out to us by Christ and by his death on the cross. In the meantime we seem to be going through a kind of germinating period in which the seed, of which St. Paul speaks as having to be first sown into the ground and die, is finding its higher purpose. Just as the acorn can only be explained in terms of the oak, so we can have our meaning only in the higher destiny for us which God must have had in mind. We are learning about love and we can learn of love only in a troubled world. That troubled world has been shared with us by God himself. And if our own troubles get too troubled entirely then the God who knows about such things through the personal experience of his Son, can always reach out and console and comfort.

We are not alone. The same Jesus who walked with his disciples in the Galilean hills, talking, explaining, calling attention to grainfields and vineyards, pointing out flowers and sparrows, chatting casually with a strange woman at the community well, visiting friends, tired, hungry, footsore – that Jesus I have finally learned is with us in our own everyday life. But more – the Jesus who was jeered, spat upon, flogged, made to stand before a mob like a clown in purple robe and thorns, crucified in the presence of his mother, despairing of his God in agony of spirit – that Jesus is also with us. There is no evil indignity and sorrow in our lives which he cannot share. Let anyone ask himself whether there is any other religion which can, even remotely offer anything like that. It is personal, meaningful, intelligent. It promises our identity and reality. It is hope for the future and courage for the present. It is Truth, it is love, it is salvation, all embodied in the one man who was the Word of God made Flesh.